Toward
More
Humanistic
Instruction

Toward More Humanistic Instruction

John A. Zahorik
The University of Wisconsin - Milwaukee

Dale L. Brubaker
The University of North Carolina at Greensboro

WM. C. BROWN COMPANY PUBLISHERS
Dubuque, Iowa

Copyright © 1972 by Wm. C. Brown Company Publishers

Library of Congress Catalog Card Number: 70—166567

ISBN 0—697—06107—8

All rights reserved. No part of this publication may be reproduced, stored in a retrieval system, or transmitted, in any form or by any means, electronic, mechanical, photocopying, recording, or otherwise, without the prior written permission of the copyright owner.

Printed in the United States of America

TO REGINA

Contents

Preface ix

PART I

A Philosophical Setting

1 The Meaning of Humanistic Education 3

PART II

Humanistic Behavior in the Classroom

2 Teacher Behavior 17
    Informing Behavior 19
    Soliciting Behavior 29
    Responding Behavior 35
    Reacting Behavior 39

3 Student Behavior 49
    Informing Behavior 51
    Soliciting Behavior 55
    Responding Behavior 57
    Reacting Behavior 59

4 The Humanistic Encounter: A Review 63
    Summarizing Humanistic Behavior 63
    The Humanistic Encounter: Transcript and Analysis 66

PART III

Making Humanistic Instruction a Reality: Content and Strategies

5 Gestalt Game Approaches 89
    Objectives 89
    Methods 94

Materials 98
Adjusting Gestalt Game Lesson Plans 103
Evaluation 110

6 Case Study Approaches 115
Student School and Community Life 116
Student Health 123
Substantive Issues 127
Conclusion 135

7 Studying Emerging Problems 137

8 Social Action Activities 145

APPENDIX

Additional Gestalt Games 153
Index 181

Preface

In recent years many writers, both professional educators who view schools from their special vantage point of experience in and knowledge about school functioning and nonprofessional educators who view schools with a unique perspective that relates schools to the broader social context in which they exist, have called attention to various forces which tend to dehumanize students in schools. They have reminded us that schools are indeed for *persons* and not for the manufacture of things. They are supposed to serve and benefit those who are compelled to spend time in them. The purpose is not to have children and youth serve schools, though this is precisely what has happened.

Although many school practices may depersonalize and alienate students, they are not a result of a conscious and deliberate effort on the part of the teachers or administrators. Often they are a result of teachers being unaware of the effects of various procedures, regulations, and techniques and of alternative courses of actions. Often the teachers are committed to more humanistic schools where the young can develop the human qualities that each possesses, but they do not know how to effect this commitment or what specific practices to use to create more humanistic education.

The purpose of this book is to move beyond general statements of the need for more *person*-oriented schools and present specific behaviors, practices, and strategies that prospective and in-service teachers can use to make humanistic instruction a reality. As the selection of content and structure reflect author biases, we have chosen to identify our biases at the onset.

1. Every decision the teacher makes has both philosophical and technical dimensions. That is, it reflects the belief system of the teacher as to what should be taught and how it can be taught most effectively. In our judgment, the teacher should be conscious of both the philosophical and technical dimensions of decision-making. Furthermore, because of the nature of the audience for whom this book is written, *we have treated both the philosophical and technical aspects of humanistic in-*

struction. Part I, Chapter 1, "The Meaning of Humanistic Education," is more philosophical than technical for in this section we prescribe a working definition of humanistic education—a definition that acts as the basis for the remainder of the book. Part II, "Humanistic Behavior in the Classroom," identifies behavior on the part of teachers and students that we have judged to be humanistic. It is both philosophical and technical. Part III, "Making Humanistic Instruction a Reality: Content and Strategies," is more technical than philosophical for, as its title indicates, it focuses on ways to begin and extend humanistic instruction.

2. In this book, we have centered our attention on the classroom setting, and (a) teacher and student behavior in this setting and (b) the subject-matter content in this setting. We recognize the fact that humanistic behavior in the classroom not only involves but depends on more than teachers and students. For example, an understanding of administrators' actions, relationships among teachers, and relationships among students is important in any analysis of classroom behavior. Other factors, such as the physical characteristics of the classroom and available instructional materials, also need to be considered. Although all of these matters are important, we focus mainly on the classroom and the interactive process and substantive material in the classroom because of our conviction that *the classroom remains the critical setting for creating humanistic instruction.*

3. We have chosen to treat subject-matter content in general rather than a particular discipline or subject field in the curriculum. We have done this because of our view that *humanistic education is not confined to any arbitrarily defined category or area.* In fact, a basic tenet of humanism, as indicated in a review of the history of the term humanism, is its emphasis on the whole man.

4. *We have not attempted to limit our writing to the analytic or value-free.* The reader will find woven throughout the entire volume the descriptive and the prescriptive, the what is and the what should be. The prescriptions that are presented have in most cases no research to support them, but this does not diminish their value. They are valid and important prescriptions because they are consistent with the meaning we give to humanism. They are a logically sound set of recommendations.

5. *We have identified elementary school teachers—prospective and in-service—as the primary audience for this book.* We have selected this group of teachers because of the need to begin humanistic education as soon as a child's school life begins and also because of the time-space flexibility that exists in elementary schools. This does not mean, however, that the prescriptions we make are not appropriate for older students.

Quite the contrary. With some translation of the numerous examples that are provided, this book is most suitable for secondary teachers.

6. *We have tried to write a book for teachers regardless of the location of their schools.* It is our position that all schools and their students can profit from new approaches that implement humanistic education. In fact, ethnocentrism is clearly incompatible with our definition of humanism.

In writing this book, we have been aided by many educators, both in the schools and at the University, and by many others. We particularly wish to thank the following: Joseph L. Frost and Joseph C. Bentley for reviewing the finished manuscript; Anna Ochoa, Grace Lund, and Robert Ubbelodhe for reading and providing valuable suggestions for various sections of the book; Arthur Baerman for the Landlord and Tenant transcript; Barbara Brubaker and Lois Zahorik for encouragement as well as welcomed advice.

Part I

A Philosophical Setting

The distinction between the theoretical and the practical, although arbitrary, is useful for analytic purposes. It is our contention that the practical daily decisions made by the teachers can be understood more clearly when viewed in a theoretical context. This context will reveal some of the basic philosophical commitments the teacher has made—consciously or otherwise.

Secondly, as authors, we have a special obligation in a book of this kind to spell out our own philosophical commitments. This we have done in the following chapter on the meaning of humanism.

CHAPTER 1

The Meaning of Humanistic Education

The clarification of terms we use has been the goal of those involved in the revolution in ethical theory. That is, contemporary moral philosophers have centered their attention on the psychology of meaning.[1] They have asked such questions as, "What do we really intend to communicate when we choose this or that word?" and "In what ways do we use words in order to elicit agreement as to our personal beliefs?" Israel Scheffler, Philosopher of Education at Harvard University, has identified three kinds of definitions which form an analytic model for viewing humanistic education.[2] The three models are stipulative, descriptive, and programmatic. In using a *stipulative* definition, one spells out or stipulates the conditions under which the term will be used for purposes of discussion. For example, the discussant might say, "When I use the term *education* in this class, I am referring to formal education." In using a *descriptive* definition, one describes the manner in which a term *is being used* in a particular context. This is essentially what a dictionary does. The describer might say, "When elementary school teachers use the term *objectives* they mean that which they expect to accomplish as a result of their teaching." In using a *programmatic* definition, one *prescribes*, that is, tells us expressly or tacitly what something *should be*. He might say, "Education is the means by which we create good citizens." What he is, in fact, saying is that he feels that education is the means by which we should create good citizens, and furthermore, others should agree with his views on this matter. It should be obvious that many definitions are a combination of the stipulative, descriptive, and programmatic.

The descriptive aspect of our definition of humanistic education is largely historical. We will on occasion refer to how men throughout history have used the term *humanism*. Our definition of humanistic education is, however, primarily stipulative and programmatic. In fact, our definition is both theme and thesis which we will follow throughout the remainder of the book.

The working model for our thesis may simply be stated, "We think humanistic behavior in the classroom is a good thing and the reader should think likewise."[3] In order to convince you that humanistic behavior in the classroom is desirable, we must first identify the characteristics of humanistic behavior in general. If we can convince you of the value of these characteristics, it logically follows that you, the reader, will "think likewise" as to the value of humanistic classroom behavior.

The aim of this chapter is to establish a philosophic base for the remainder of the book. The fact that we intend to define humanistic behavior in somewhat general terms in this chapter may at times be disquieting to the reader. We would urge you to read on, for Part II, "Humanistic Behavior in the Classroom," gives very specific examples of humanistic behavior. Let us now proceed to philosophic commitments that we consider to be characteristics of humanistic behavior in general.

1. The all-encompassing value espoused by humanists is that *all people have worth or value by virtue of being human.* In other words, the fundamental standard of human conduct is the *dignity of man.*[4] This statement is not aimed at minimizing the uniqueness of each individual. To the contrary, it is aimed at developing each individual to his full ability. It is simply to say that all behavior should be judged ". . . by the extent to which it contributes to human dignity and respect for the individual."[5] Another way to express this idea is to say that humanists are opposed to that which would threaten to destroy both man and nature. Environmental violence, such as pollution, serves as an obvious example. Racism is another example, for it not only threatens man directly but also threatens nature, as evidenced in impacted housing patterns in our cities. In our judgment, these problems and others should be an important part of the subject matter for any class in the elementary school curriculum.

Admittedly, our statements regarding the dignity of man as the fundamental standard of human conduct are general, thus indicating their all-encompassing nature. It is therefore encumbent on us to give them more specific meaning. This we will do as we move on to more concrete characteristics. (Terms such as "good citizenship," "patriotism," and "inquiry" are justly criticized, not because they are used but because their characteristics are too obscure.)

2. Humanistic behavior is based on the optimistic tenet that *man can make a difference in improving the quality of life.** This belief has historically pitted humanists against *some* religious followers who feel

---

*To define man as Homo esperans—the hoping man—is to say that man has a basic need, psychological in nature, to be able to look forward to better times.

that man's lot is predetermined and/or divine intervention will be the answer to man's problems. In short, humanists reject asceticism in any form. Or in the words of Protagoras, man is "the measure of all things." To say that man is the architect of his own destiny is both optimistic and awesome. It obviously entails both freedom and responsibility. And yet, the statement appears to be especially true in a century that has produced men as different as Adolf Hitler and Martin Luther King, Jr.

3. A closely related belief comes to us from classical humanism: *man is capable of rational and reflective thought and will be freed by knowledge derived from the use of these qualities.*[6] One may immediately retort by saying that man is also capable of irrational thought as evidenced by a parade of twentieth-century dictators.* Of course this is true. What the humanist is actually saying is that man *should use* rational reflective thought in order to improve the quality of existence.

A nearly exclusive reliance on rational thought by some humanists has caused some action-oriented critics to reject humanism. It is the detached, idealistic stance which falls short of action that is under fire at this time in the history of industrially-advanced nations. Youth in particular have challenged yesterday's humanists to eliminate the gap between idealistic rhetoric and action. At the same time, many young romantics have little interest in rational and reflective thought.[7] We see the greatest challenge to twentieth-century humanism in this area. That is, a new humanism must give fair play to both rational thought and man's feelings and his actions. (Classroom strategies discussed in Part III of this book are aimed at meeting this challenge.) There is precedent for emphasis on reason, feelings, and actions in the development of humanism. Classical humanists designed a curriculum for the whole man—a curriculum that was aimed at developing students' minds, emotions, and bodies. One of the best examples of this total approach

---

*Some phenomenologists criticize humanism for failing to see that man's capacity for evil is an essential rather than accidental part of his nature. For example, see Lionel Rubinoff, *The Pornography of Power*, (New York: Ballantine Books, 1969). In our view the essential fact is that man is capable of both good and evil. At any rate, the humanist's faith in man's rational being is not a denial of man's irrational capabilities. Instead, it is a plea for the transcendence of such irrationality. To the extent that man denies such irrationality we may say that his behavior is pornographic. Using the denial of the irrationality of power as an example, we may say that "just as the repression of sex leads to sexual fantasies and sexual perversions, so the repression of the irrationality of power leads not only to the *fantasy* of power but also to the corrupt behavior which is the *exercise of power.*" *Ibid.*, p. 6. By *exercise of power* we mean the indiscriminate use of power for one's own ego gratification.

To say that man is both rational and irrational is to say that he is ambivalent. "He seeks to be what he is not and not to be what he is; he is a being whose very being emerges through self-negation. From this concept we can better appreciate man's capacity for evil." *Ibid.*, p. 9.

to education today is found in the liberal arts curriculum of most colleges and universities. Courses in art, music, and physical education are required of all students in the interest of developing the whole man.

4. Although science does not embrace the whole of human experience, *humanists have seen science as the most important instrument fashioned by man.*[8] The term *instrument* is carefully chosen for science is considered to be nonmoral. Those with the power of scientific knowledge in their hands determine whether it will be used as an instrument for construction or destruction. It is precisely because of the powerful influence of science that humanists emphasize the moral responsibility that accompanies it. We feel that one of the most pressing subjects for elementary school students is the use of scientific know-how. If we name the most important problems facing our nation and world, we can immediately see that science has had and will continue to play an important role. Urban housing, race relations, pollution, and the population explosion serve as examples.

Although humanists placed great faith in science, they strongly rejected the dehumanizing and depersonalizing effects of the technological revolution. In fact, twentieth-century humanism can be understood in large measure as a response to the complexities of industrial life.* This response came largely in the form of social reforms. A representative document of the humanistic spirit of this age is George S. Counts' *The Selective Character of American Secondary Education* (1922). Counts was clearly on the side of the less "well-to-do" classes as he accused high schools of perpetuating racial, social class, and ethnic inequalities. In particular, Counts decried the lack of opportunities for children of laborers. Counts placed a great faith for the alleviation of these ills in organized labor. (The conservative nature of much of organized labor today lends itself to an ironic view of Counts' faith. At the same time, Counts' position should be viewed in terms of the conditions that existed when he made his prescriptions.)

We see one of the strongest challenges to humanistic education today in relation to the advanced stages the technological revolution has taken. Alienation is a response to organized hugeness—a response that teachers must deal with each day in their classrooms. The stability zones of yesterday are gone. We feel that pupils should understand this revolution and find creative alternatives to meet their psychological needs. Teaching strategies in Part III are designed to deal with this issue.

---

*Erich Fromm labels this era as the second Industrial Revolution. Human thought is being replaced by the thinking of machines (computers). *The Revolution of Hope* (New York: Bantam Books, 1968), p. 27. "Loss of Identity" is the subject of some materials included in Part III of our book.

5. The hope that science offers leads us to another important characteristic of humanistic behavior. Humanistic behavior should be evidence of man's commitment to *understanding and alleviating the plight of the oppressed*. As in the words of Michael Harrington, the "haves" clearly have an obligation to aid the "have nots."

To say that the "haves" have an obligation to aid the "have nots" is immediately suspect to many who have suffered from the paternalism of *some* "*haves*."* It is at this point that we must differentiate between the obligation "haves" have in aiding "have nots" and the manner in which such aid is given. This distinction is clearly made in Michael Harrington's *The Other America*. In this book we do not shy away from the obligation "haves" have toward "have nots." In our view the "missionary" position depends on "what one is selling" and "how it is sold."

An important responsibility the humanist has in understanding and alleviating the plight of the oppressed is to *communicate* that which he has learned so that others may profit from the experience. This obligation has its roots in classical humanism as exemplified in the allegory of the cave from Plato's *Republic*. The unfettered "educated" man who left the cave and saw the light had a moral obligation to return to teach those in darkness.

Communication involves more than the words exchanged between people. The emotional or affective dimension of the communicative process is reflected in tone of voice, eye contact, and body movement as well as in the words that are used. And so we can say that the implications of this aspect of humanistic education are many and varied. We intend to focus on communication, especially between teacher and students, in Parts II and III of this book.

The interesting thing about communication is the mutuality achieved between parties when it is used effectively. Such mutuality has important moral implications in conflict resolution—certainly an important aim in this age of confrontation and conflict.

6. *Humanistic behavior reflects a pragmatic, problem-solving orientation.*[9] By this we mean that humanists are committed to solving practical problems. Other worldly matters are not the concern of the humanist. The proper focus for a humanistic curriculum is the tackling of contemporary problems facing our nation and peoples throughout the world. Population growth, urbanization, and environmental violence are but

---

*Many universities, for example, no longer refer to community service but instead use a term such as *community involvement*. This is especially true in urban areas sensitive to paternalism toward minority groups—especially blacks. The land grant service terminology is still quite acceptable when used in regard to white farmers in nonurban areas.

three examples of problems that should be an important part of the elementary school curriculum. At the same time that we identify such problems as *subject matter,* we hasten to add that problem solving is an investigative *process* that should be stimulated by formal schooling. The process, however, is a lifelong process not limited to formal education. (This was in part what John Dewey meant by the term *growth.*)

An essential part of the problem-solving process is the problem-solver's *curiosity* or *inquisitiveness.* This curiosity is evidence that the inquirer feels the importance of solving the problem or minimizing the doubt in his mind.

Problem solving is also the inquiry process whereby the individual, after reaching a forked-road situation, suggests alternative solutions (hypotheses) and then pursues such alternatives in the light of his own value system.

A comprehensive discussion of problem solving as an inquiry process is found in Parts II and III of this book, but for the moment we want to leave the reader with a sense of the spirit of the process.

7. Although humanism emphasizes one's responsibility to his nation, chauvinism is clearly in opposition to man's concern for the dignity of *all* men. In a more positive vein, it can be said that *contemporary humanism has an important international dimension to it.* The problems that face one nation are the concern of all men. Overpopulation serves as an example. Likewise, the successes of one nation, as evidenced in space achievements, are the concern of all men. A humanistic education is one that is internationally minded. The materials we have developed in Part III have such a goal in mind.

8. *Humanism that is relevant to our times must squarely face values in conflict.* There can be no denying that our age is one of confrontation and conflict. The mass media have not only brought such conflict to the surface but in the process of doing so have stimulated further conflict. Our cities have burned and our university campuses have been shut down. Those who support humanism cannot ignore such realities but must instead deal with them head-on.

9. Contemporary humanism must come to grips with the *relationship between power and morality,* idealism and reality, what is and what should be. At present "might makes right" is more than a cliché; it is a reality. Might can be defined in terms of control over the lives of others —control often in the form of propaganda so that he "who holds the instruments of propaganda such as television and the press is not only powerful but 'right.' The replacement of absolute standards as to what is right by the relativistic view that one's perception is all important

supports the view that he who controls perceptions of people through the mass media is both powerful and "right."

In the process of dealing with the concept of power, a relevant humanism must treat the relationship between the individual and the group. Humanists assert that one's self-concept is enhanced by asking "Who Am I?" which is what Socrates meant when he said that the unexamined life is not worth living. At the same time that such individual and personal questions are crucial, we must look at groups of people as organic bodies in themselves and institutionalize changes that are humanizing. The relationship between the one and the many is more than philosophical, for to move from the one to the many is to use that power that is available to realize one's wishes.

10. Emphasis on the individual and his self-concept indicates the *humanist's interest in man's psychological and emotional life.* We must ask the question "How Can Man Maintain the Proper Emotional and Psychological Stability in an Age of Conflict and Rapid Change?" Seventeenth-century humanists claimed that the virtuous life would necessarily make man feel better. If today's humanist squarely faces the many problems in this age of conflict he may very well feel worse. At any rate, the relationship between conflict and stability is crucial and deserves our attention.

11. Finally, all that we have said about humanism indicates that it is largely qualitative rather than quantitative. This is to say that *effectiveness*, a qualitative term, is more important than *efficiency*. Efficiency is based on the assumption that increased *production* ("the more the better") and therefore *consumption* should be the modus operandi of any society. The result of this seductive but misleading style of life is that man's role becomes largely mechanical and passive.

Notes

1. For a summary and analysis of the contributions of linguistic analysts G. E. Moore, Charles L. Stevenson, Stephen Toulmin, and R. M. Hare, see George C. Kerner, *The Revolution in Ethical Theory* (London: Oxford University Press, 1966).
2. Israel Scheffler, *The Language of Education* (Springfield, Illinois: Charles C. Thomas, 1960), pp. 11-35.
3. Charles L. Stevenson, *Ethics and Language* (New Haven, Conn.: Yale University Press, 1960), p. 21. Stevenson's model reads as follows: "This is good" means *I approve of this; do so as well.*
4. Donald W. Oliver and James P. Shaver, *Teaching Public Issues in the High School* (Boston: Houghton Mifflin Co., 1966), p. 59.
5. *Ibid.* The authors discuss problems involved in subscribing to this general statement and then give more specific meaning to the prescription. James B.

Macdonald makes a useful distinction between the individual and the person. The uniqueness of individuals is a commonly accepted idea in curriculum and instruction. The person, on the other hand, is valued because of what he holds in common and therefore shares with other persons, "The Person in the Curriculum." Speech delivered at the 1965 Teachers College Curriculum Conference, Columbia University, November 9, 1965, pp. 3-5. What Macdonald is saying is that our respect for what all persons hold in common is the "cement" or faith that allows us to trust and support individuals' differences.

6. For a brief discussion of classical, Christian, and social(ist) humanism, see James B. Macdonald, "The High School in Human Terms: Curriculum Design." N. K. Hamilton and J. G. Saylor eds., *Humanizing the Secondary School* (Washington, D. C.: Association for Supervision and Curriculum Development, 1969), pp. 36-7.

7. This point was made by Richard Whittemore, "By Inquiry Alone?" *Social Education.* March 1970, Vol. 34, No. 3, p. 282. "The effort to subject ideals, beliefs, and questions of public morality to the canons of logic and scientific method is probably more offensive to young romantics than the most old-fashioned attempts to teach them history or government. At least the latter do not assault their faith in the private vision. Often, for them, logic and system are the mortal enemies of understanding, especially in the emotion-charged areas of private and public morality." *Ibid.*, pp. 282-3.

8. George S. Counts. *Education and American Civilization* (New York: Bureau of Publications, Teachers College, Columbia University, 1952), pp. 244-58.

9. The relationship between humanism and pragmatism is explored by F. C. S. Schiller, "Humanism." *Encyclopedia of the Social Sciences*, E. R. A. Seligman and A. Johnson, eds., (New York: The Macmillan Co., 1957), pp. 542-3. In 1903, Charles S. Peirce proposed to William James the term *humanism* to describe the philosophic movement started by James in 1900. James replied that it was too late to use *humanism* in place of *pragmatism* although he realized the merits of such a transition. We can therefore see that the terms were nearly interchangeable and continue to be so to many philosophers to this day.

Part II

Humanistic Behavior in the Classroom

There is no paucity of statements concerning the meaning of humanism for actual educational practices. Many have called attention to nonhumanistic behaviors and events found in schools, described what a humanistic education would be like, and urged teachers and administrators to create more humanistic schools. Combs has done this forcefully.[1] He calls attention to a list of dehumanizing practices and conditions found in schools and developed by the ASCD Commission on Humanism in Education. The list included the following:

1. The marking system and
   a. The competition it inspires
   b. The comparisons it makes
   c. The pressure it creates
   d. Failure
2. Corporal punishment
3. Overcrowding and resulting
   a. Class loads
   b. Easy anonymity
   c. Shallow teacher-pupil relationships
   d. Loss of privacy
4. Curricular tracking and
   a. The caste system it nurtures
5. Inflexible and nonvariable time schedules
6. The scarcity of legitimate postgraduate options and
   a. Pressure to attend college
7. The "single text" approach and
   a. The conformity it demands
   b. The boredom it creates
8. The grade-level lock-step which ignores what we know about the ways in which unique selves develop and
   a. Accompanying imposition of single scope and sequence schemes
9. Misuse and misinterpretation of intelligence, achievement, and aptitude tests
10. Testing instead of evaluating
11. Teacher evaluation of students
12. Failure to reflect teacher responsibility for grade or mark "achieved" by students
13. The "objectivity model" which prevents meaningful relationships from developing between teachers and pupils
14. The ignoring of the principle of "feedback readiness"
15. The "right" answer syndrome
16. Misuse of cumulative records
17. Demonstrated distrust instead of demonstrated faith.[2]

To bring about humanistic education, Combs would have us change the primary focus of education from that of acquiring knowledge or experience to that of discovering the personal meaning of information. Personal meaning is a humanistic goal; knowledge or information as a goal is impersonal and nonhumanistic. The following are suggestions offered by Combs to develop personal meaning and create humanistic education in our schools: (1) de-emphasize information and objectivity; (2) value personal meaning of students; (3) accept students for what they are; (4) encourage personal exploration and discovery of personal meaning through individualized, flexible, self-directed learning experiences; (5) evaluate and reward students on the basis of the meanings they have rather than on what they know; and (6) recognize and reward teachers for their efforts to produce humanistic students.

These representative statements relative to making schooling more humanistic as well as identifying present dehumanizing practices that pervade education are important statements and contribute significantly to achieving the goal of humanistic education. These statements and others concerning humanistic education are not as helpful as they could be, however, because of their generalness. For the statements to be of use to teachers, administrators, and others, they need to be much more specific. If we are to value personal meaning or de-emphasize information we need to know specifically how to do these things. We need to know what planning is necessary, what classroom behaviors to employ, what materials to use, how to organize students. If we are to eliminate the single text or rigid time schedules we have to know what replacements we can use and how they function. Without specificity, particularly without specificity in terms of teacher behaviors, suggestions for making humanistic education a reality may be sterile.

In addition to making the statements more specific, greater balance in the types of statements made would be facilitating. It appears that a majority of the statements about dehumanizing school practices are organization or school system functioning oriented. Organization is an important variable in developing humanistic education, but intraclassroom prescriptions relative to curriculum and instruction are more valuable because they focus on areas over which teachers have considerable influence. More and specific prescriptions in the areas of curriculum and instruction are essential if humanistic education is to exist and grow.

It is a major function of this book to translate pronouncements about humanism into detailed classroom curriculum and instructional practices. The term "curriculum," as used here, refers to plans for future action that take place prior to instruction.[3] It includes subject-matter content as well as student-learning experiences, materials, evaluative devices. Instruction refers to the teaching-learning context in which the curriculum is implemented. It refers to the specific teacher behaviors and student behaviors that occur within the classroom as the teacher attempts to bring about learning on the part of the student. Both of these areas are significant in creating humanistic education because humanism is both content and process, substance and procedures, material and format.

In this section instruction is discussed. Curriculum is dealt with in the following section along with strategies for making humanistic education a reality. Instruction is singled out for separate treatment here because of the writers' belief that instruction has not received just attention in the past. McLuhan's hypothesis that the medium is the message may be an overstatement.[4] But, certainly the notion that the medium is *a* message and, quite possibly the dominant message, is not without validity. Applied to education, this means that instruction or what the teachers and students actually do in classrooms as they interact with each other is the major learning outcome for students. What they learn is what happens to them to a greater extent than what they are told. For humanistic education in which man's worth and dignity are respected, his individual uniqueness enhanced, his problem-solving talents recognized, and his rational thought abilities extended, the process of education or instruction becomes a primary concern.

To identify and examine humanistic instructional behavior on the part of the teachers and students, a model of instruction based on Bellack's pedagogical moves is employed.[5] This model consists of four pedagogical acts that can be used by either teachers or students. They are informing, soliciting, responding, and reacting. Informing consists of structuring or setting the context for the teaching and learning that is to follow and relating or making substantive statements of fact, opinion, or belief. Soliciting refers to questions, commands, or requests that elicit verbal or physical responses. The responding act fulfills the expectation of the solicitation, while the reacting act rates or attempts to develop the response. Humanistic teacher behaviors in relation to this model are presented and analyzed in Chapter 2. In Chapter 3, student behaviors in relation to the model are discussed. Chapter 4 presents a summary and unification of these classroom behaviors.

Throughout this section of the book the terms humanistic and nonhumanistic behavior are used. These terms should not be interpreted as discrete elements but rather as ranges of more or less humanism at the two ends of a continuum of humanistic behavior. The term humanistic behavior should be viewed as a behavior that is in the direction of humanism and that is more humanistic than nonhumanistic. Similarly, the term nonhumanistic behavior should be viewed as a behavior that is in the opposite direction of humanism, that is more nonhumanistic than humanistic.

Notes

1. Arthur W. Combs, "An Educational Imperative: The Humane Dimension." *To Nurture Humaneness: Commitment for the '70's.* The 1970 Yearbook of the Association for Supervision and Curriculum Development (Washington, D. C.: The Association, 1970), pp. 173-188.

2. *Ibid.*, p. 179.

3. James B. Macdonald, "Education Models for Instruction—Introduction." *Theories of Instruction*, ed. James B. Macdonald and Robert R. Leeper (Washington, D. C.: Association for Supervision and Curriculum Development, 1965), pp. 1-7.

4. Marshall McLuhan and Quentin Fiore, *The Medium is the Massage* (New York: Bantam Books, 1967).

5. Arno A. Bellack, *et al.*, *The Language of the Classroom* (New York: Teachers College Press, 1966).

Teacher Behavior

CHAPTER 2

As teachers interact with students during the course of instruction they display a great variety and number of verbal and nonverbal behaviors. They ask questions, rate students' answers, state facts and opinions, give directions, clarify students' remarks, repeat answers, and engage in countless other behaviors. Some of these behaviors are humanistic or can be used humanistically, while others dehumanize and degrade students. Before those teacher behaviors that are humanistic can be identified and examined, it is necessary to clarify the goal of humanistic teacher behavior and to suggest a list of criteria that must be met for the teacher behavior to be labeled humanistic.

The goal of humanistic teacher behavior in the instructional setting is to permit, encourage, and extend students' ability to be independent, self-directed, responsible persons. It is to inspire and aid each student in his effort to develop those human qualities that he possesses: thinking, feeling, valuing, and symbol-creating.[1] Teacher behavior that thrusts students into dependent, passive roles in which real thought and real values are not only unaccepted but are actually discouraged is not humanistic. The aim of humanistic teacher behavior must be student freedom, freedom to become increasingly more human.

Criteria for humanistic teacher behavior that emerge from this goal are the following. For teacher classroom behavior to be humanistic it must be:

1. Receptive

    Teacher behavior must be open and receptive to students' ideas, feelings, and actions. It must encourage and be willing to deal with those matters that concern students. If the behavior is restrictive and closed, independent thinking, valuing, and acting will be discouraged.

2. Facilitating

    Teacher behavior must not only be receptive to students' ideas, it must also facilitate students' thinking and valuing. It must help students to develop those human characteristics each possesses. Perhaps the term "service" as used by Huebner best expresses this criterion.[2] He states that if schools are to be moral institutions they need to be of service to individuals. Schools need to serve the full range of interests and talents of students. Students should not be asked to serve the school.

3. Personal

    The behaviors that the teacher uses in accepting and developing students' ideas cannot be stereotyped and routinized. The exact same behavior usually cannot be used with all students. Humanistic teacher behaviors are individual and unique for each student. They must be sensitive and responsive to the interests, needs, and talents of each student.

4. Genuine

    As well as being personal the behavior of the teacher must be genuine, honest, and sincere. Superficial openness and service will not lead to greater humanism on the part of students. Teachers must be deeply interested in the lives of students and this interest and genuine concern must be manifested in the teachers' behavior.

These criteria are similar to the attitudes that Rogers identifies as facilitating experiential learning.[3] He defines experiential learning as meaningful learning that is self-initiated, pervasive, has a quality of personal involvement, and is self-evaluated. The attitudes are realness, acceptance, and empathy. Realness means meeting students on a person-to-person basis. It means being oneself. Prizing the student as an imperfect human being with many potentialities is what Rogers means by acceptance. Empathy refers to understanding the student from the student's point of view. With these attitudes the teacher can be a great aid to student learning.

Another point closely related to the fourth criterion for humanistic teacher behavior that needs to be stated before discussing specific teacher behaviors is the teacher as a person. For the teacher to be successful in his efforts to permit and encourage student humanism, he must be a humanist himself, both in school and out of school. He must exemplify and value the humanistic man. He must employ behavior "which displays thinking, expresses and struggles with values, expresses feelings, and demonstrates creative and playful manipulation of symbols."[4] In other words, the teacher must be what Kelley,[5] Rogers,[6] and others call a fully functioning person.

The discussion can now turn to the identification and examination of specific humanistic behaviors of teachers. As a framework for viewing humanistic teacher behavior a model of teaching derived from Bellack's pedagogical moves is used because its elements are quite discrete and it is both a simple and encompassing model.[7] Types and patterns of teacher humanistic behavior are treated in relation to each of the four elements of the model: informing, soliciting, responding, and reacting.

Informing Behavior

Informing is a behavior in which all teachers engage. It is composed of two subbehaviors: structuring and relating. Structuring can be defined as those acts which establish the setting in which teaching and learning will occur. Relating refers to the stating of substantive facts, generalizations, opinions, values, ideas, and the like. Each of these subbehaviors is explored in turn.

Several researchers have examined, either directly or indirectly, structuring behavior and have attempted to describe it. Perhaps the most extensive analysis has been done by Bellack and his associates.[8] In a study which conceptualizes teaching as a language game and attempts to come to understand the meanings that are communicated in the various verbal behaviors of the players at the secondary school level, Bellack identifies ten dimensions to the structuring act:

1. Function

    Function refers to the general type of structuring act performed. It can be launching in which some activity or topic is started, or it can be halting-excluding in which the activity or topic is terminated.

2. Method

    Method refers to how the launching or halting-excluding is carried out. It can be done by simply announcing what is to follow or by stating a proposition. A proposition deals with subject matter in an analytic, empirical, or evaluative way.

3. Activity

    Activity refers to the kind of verbal or nonverbal performance to be carried on. It can be general oral, discussing, reporting, questioning-answering, reading, and others.

4. Agent

   Agent refers to who will perform the activity. It can be the total class, the teacher only, a small group of students, and others.

5. Topic

   Topic refers to the content of the discourse. It can deal with subject matter or classroom management.

6. Logical Process

   Logical process refers to the cognitive processes involved in dealing with the topic. It can be defining, interpreting, explaining, evaluating, and others.

7. Time

   Time refers to when the activity will begin and how long it will last.

8. Regulations

   Regulations refer to rules by which the activity is carried out. It deals with such aspects as scope of topic, time sequence, and administrative matters.

9. Instructional Aids

   Instructional aids refer to materials to be used in the activity such as books, maps, films, and outlines.

10. Reasons

    Reasons refer to giving an explanation as to why a certain activity is to follow.

Hughes also examined structuring behavior in the classroom although not as intensively as Bellack.[9] The purpose of Hughes' investigation was to try to determine a method of rating teachers. To do this she focused on the functions teachers perform for students. One of the functions that she identified has two subfunctions that deal with structuring: one is termed structure and the other regulate. Structure, as Hughes defines it, refers to the announcing of the area of attention. It can be a topic, problem, or activity. Some of the types of structuring with accompanying examples are:

1. Open Structure

   The area of attention is given without calling for a single, correct response, e.g., "Today we'll talk about what interests you most in the story."

2. Closed Structure

    The response is limited to one precise answer, e.g., "For the rest of the period we're going to review our number facts."

3. Oriented Structure

    The relationship of new content to previously studied material is pointed out, e.g., "Now that we've studied Wisconsin's agriculture, let's examine their industry."

4. Public Criteria Structure

    The reasons for the particular activity, problem, or topic are stated, e.g., "Let's review these words. I'm not sure we all know them."

Regulate, according to Hughes, refers to indicating who is to be involved in the activity or what the order of action will be. Several of Hughes' types of regulate with accompanying examples are:

1. Open Regulate

    Anyone can respond and there is no particular order in which the action will proceed, e.g., "Anyone who wishes to may collect the books."

2. Closed Regulate

    No alternative as to who is to respond or to the order of action is given, e.g., "Jane, take this to the office."

3. Neutral Regulate

    The order of response is done in a way that gives everyone an equal chance to respond, e.g., "Let's begin in alphabetical order."

4. Public Criteria Regulate

    The reasons for who is to respond or for the action to be taken is given, e.g., "Tom, you do that one; you need practice with subtraction."

For a third examination of structuring behavior readers are directed to the work of Taba and her colleagues on thinking in classrooms, which is described in the section on reacting behavior.[10] What she calls focusing is essentially structuring behavior.

Some structuring behaviors or ways of structuring are humanistic and others are not. Some are more receptive, facilitating, personal, and genuine, and others more restrictive, discouraging, impersonal, and superficial. A majority of the structuring behaviors may not meet all of the criteria for humanistic teacher behavior nor any of the criteria.

Nevertheless, it is possible to identify specific behaviors and behavioral patterns that are primarily humanistic or primarily nonhumanistic.

What is humanistic structuring behavior and nonhumanistic structuring behavior of teachers? First of all, for structuring behavior to be humanistic, there has to be less of it in total. Bellack and his associates found that structuring behavior accounted for 7.7 per cent of the teachers' behaviors and 20.1 per cent of the teachers' spoken lines in secondary teaching. This usage is far too extensive. It is too extensive for the secondary school and also for the elementary school where it probably exists in similar proportions. From a humanistic standpoint structuring behavior of teachers needs to be decreased because it restricts student self-direction and independence. It makes students dependent on the teacher for direction. Extensive structuring by the teacher denies students' rationality and problem-solving capabilities. Although some teacher structuring is essential to classroom functioning, a considerable amount of teacher structuring should be replaced by teacher-student cooperative structuring and student self-structuring. Student self-structuring is discussed in greater detail in Chapter 3.

Secondly, for that teacher structuring behavior that is essential to be humanistic, it should contain few of the ten dimensions identified by Bellack, and those that are present should be open and permit variation in student behavior. Some of the dimensions that should not be used if possible or should be general if they are necessary are the agent, time, regulations, and aids. These aspects of structuring can often be withheld from any structuring move. When they are withheld, students are faced with freedom and choices. They must make decisions for themselves. When these dimensions are absent, everyone can participate in the activity, for whatever time span the task demands, with any aids or restrictions they consider to be helpful. Students also have to rely on self-direction if some of the remaining dimensions are general rather than specific. Structuring behavior in which the activity is general oral, the topic is broad, and the logical process is high level calls for considerable student initiative. Students must decide for themselves in what activity they will engage and with what specific substantive topic they will deal. Evaluative or explanation logical processes demand more student independent thought than definition. This structuring is far more humanistic than that in which these dimensions are painstakingly laid out. Also, structuring in which the method is stating a proposition and reasons for the activity are presented is humanistic because it appeals to students' thinking ability. Structuring that launches is more humanistic than structuring that halts or excludes because launching carries the promise of stimulating and interesting students while halting-excluding often ends topics of interest to students.

In Hughes' terms the structuring that is humanistic is the structure and regulate that is open and provides public criteria. Open structure and open regulate in which there is great freedom in content to be pursued and in who is permitted to pursue it are humanistic because again students are allowed to exercise self-control and make decisions for themselves. Closed structure and closed regulate in which there is no freedom in content nor in who is to respond are nonhumanistic. Public criteria, like reasons, are a humanistic ingredient of structuring because of their tacit recognition of students' rationality.

The following are examples of teacher humanistic structuring behavior:

1. Let's give some thought now to the causes of the decline in population of many of our major cities as indicated in preliminary 1970 census reports. Let's try to get at some of the possible reasons.
2. We all know that automobile exhaust is an important cause of air pollution in our cities. The devices put on cars in recent years to decrease engine pollutants have not been effective. Automobiles, trucks, and buses continue to pollute, but yet we need them for our society to function. This is really a problem. I'm sure many of us have possible solutions.
3. Since most everyone has been having some difficulty with these fractions, I think it would be a good idea to review them.
4. Let's focus on your reactions to visiting the hospital. Let's discuss what interested you most.

Not all of these examples meet all of the preceding suggestions concerning humanistic teacher structuring, but each meets most of them. The first one does not include time, regulation, or aids, the agent is not given or at least it is regulate-open, the activity is general, the process is high level, and it is a launching move. The topic, however, is not as broad as some topics are, the behavior is not a proposition, and no reasons or public criteria are given. The second example is very similar to the first in dimensions except that it is a proposition. The third example does not indicate time, regulation, or aids, the activity is general, it launches, and a reason or public criterion is given for the activity. The agent, although indicated, is still general; any or all students can be involved. It is not a proposition, the topic is fairly narrow, and the cognitive process is fairly low level, however. The last example does not provide reasons and is not a proposition, but it is extremely open in terms of activity, topic, and process. The agent is given but, again, it is open.

In contrast to these examples, the following are examples of nonhumanistic structuring:

1. For the next hour I'd like everyone to work the addition problems on page 170 of the text.
2. Today, boys and girls, I would like you to report on the five major causes of racial discrimination. Let's only deal with current ones that we've read about and can substantiate. Please try to keep your reports down to a few minutes.
3. I'm sorry, boys, we can't go into that now. It's an interesting idea, but it is pretty far afield from what we should be doing. Perhaps when we study France we can deal with it.

These structuring behaviors are considered nonhumanistic for several reasons. The agent is usually given, time and regulations are indicated, the activity is specific, topics are less broad, the process is not high level, and no propositions nor reasons are used. The first two launch, but the last one halts-excludes. With these three structuring behaviors student independence and self-direction are thoroughly discouraged.

Before proceeding to relating, the other aspect of informing, there is one additional matter concerning structuring that should be discussed. Perhaps many readers are saying to themselves at this point that they use and have been taught to use structuring behaviors that are more similar to the second set of examples rather than the first. The examples in the second set are more specific, more detailed, more exact, and, therefore, are useful to students. The response to this thought is that from the standpoint of developing humanistic students, specific, detailed structuring simply is not helpful. There may be several occasions where it is wise to use more closed, specific structure for a short time, but over the long run, structuring must be open and general. One of these occasions is when students, either individually or in groups, directly solicit teacher structuring. Another is when a teacher is having difficulty in managing the classroom. Closed, specific structuring can be very effective in controlling a group of students that lacks self-discipline. If closed structure is used in these situations, the teacher must as quickly as possible after the class has been brought under control attempt more open structuring so that students can develop the humanistic qualities they possess. A third occasion is for an activity that needs organization to get underway, such as a simulation game.

Relating is the second aspect of informing to be examined. Relating, to review, refers to substantive statements of fact, opinion, value, explanation, inference, causality, analysis, interpretation, and other similar kinds of pronouncements. It can be a lengthy behavior lasting for more than thirty minutes or it can be quite short lasting for only a second or two. It is a behavior that is not issued in direct response to a question or in direct reaction to a response. It is an initiatory behavior rather than a reflexive one. When a teacher relates he makes informational statements about subject-matter content or process that he had planned to make prior to the beginning of the teaching-learning situation or that he decides during the class session to make because they are consistent with the purposes of the class session. Answering students' questions is not relating unless the teacher goes beyond the requested response and begins to provide unsolicited analyses or ideas. Developing or extending a student's response is also not relating unless the teacher interjects and expands facts or opinions that clearly go beyond the student's response.

Although even the casual observer of the instructional act is aware of the fact that a very large portion of teaching consists of relating, there does not seem to be much research on this behavior. Several investigators identify it and provide data relative to its use, but thorough analysis of its elements or dimensions is lacking.

Smith and Meux identify it in their study on logical operations of teaching.[11] To examine the logical aspects of teaching, or the forms teacher verbal behavior takes in developing subject matter and which can be evaluated by reference to rules of validity and correctness, Smith and Meux developed two types of units: episode and monologue. The episode consisting of an opening phase, a continuing phase, and a closing phase formed the basis for the examination of logical operations. The monologue which was not analyzed extensively is very similar to relating behavior. The monologue, according to Smith and Meux, is a solo performance of a speaker addressing a group. It is usually found in the didactic or expository discourse of the teacher and often displays paragraph-to-paragraph progression. In monologue discourse the speaker usually moves from point to point in his remarks, presenting it, elaborating on it, and then proceeding to some other point.

Relating is also identified in the Verbal Interaction Category System developed by Amidon and Hunter.[12] It is the first category of their seventeen category system which expands the Flanders System.[13] The category is titled Gives Information or Opinion. It refers to short remarks or extended lecturing of the teacher that presents content, ideas, explanations, orientations, or rhetorical questions. At present specific analyses of this behavior are not available.

Perhaps the most detailed treatment of relating was done by the Wisconsin Teacher Education Research Project.[14] They developed a system for analyzing communication acts in the classroom that is based on a system created by Lewis and others.[15] This instrument contains a number of categories that are relating behaviors:

1. Gives academically verifiable information.
2. Gives information about past, present, or future experiences of one student or a small group of students.
3. Gives information about past, present, or future experiences of the total class.
4. Gives objective information within a personal frame of reference for a student, small group, or the total class.
5. Gives information about an experience of the teacher.
6. Gives suggestion about action or indicates alternatives.
7. Gives personal opinion, personal interpretation, or expresses feelings about subject matter.
8. Gives personal opinion or personal interpretation, or expresses feelings about things not related to subject matter.
9. Gives analysis of a topic under discussion by referring to a point of view or criterion that is explicitly stated and not the teacher's personal point of view.

In a longitudinal study concerning the communication behavior of university instructors and elementary teachers as student teachers and as full-time teachers it was found that a considerable portion of teaching time is spent in relating. The university professors used it from 66 to 31 per cent of the time, depending on the specific instructional approach being employed. The mean use of the elementary teachers was approximately 27 per cent. Of the subcategories of this behavior, those having to do with giving information were used the most frequently.

All of these researchers provide interesting and useful information concerning relating behavior such as relating often occurs in paragraph form, it can be for individuals or groups, it can take the form of opinion or analysis, and giving information is the most frequently used kind of relating. What is perhaps the most significant aspect of relating from the standpoint of humanistic teaching is not investigated, however. From this standpoint, the function or purpose for which the relating behavior is being used is the important aspect. All teachers must issue opinions, facts, and analyses to some degree. What makes this relating behavior humanistic or nonhumanistic is primarily not the specific type employed, but the purpose for which the teacher employed it.

For teacher relating behavior to be humanistic its purpose must be to (1) familiarize students with topics or areas that are new to them and in which they can identify personally significant problems to pursue, or (2) facilitate students' inquiry after they have identified problems or clarified goals.

Relating behavior that performs the function of familiarizing students with various events and topics consists of analyses, facts, judgments, inferences, and other types of relating. Its chief aim is to expose, stimulate, and interest students. It seeks to ignite students' curiosity so that they begin to raise questions which they may wish to attempt to resolve. Relating behavior that familiarizes is neither didactic nor insistent. Its purpose is not to have all students acquire some particular learning. It simply presents a great variety and number of facts, concepts, ideas, and the like which individual students may "pick up and run with" or may ignore.

Relating behavior that familiarizes is humanistic because it is both receptive and personal. It is receptive because it invites students' interests. Its goal is to get students to identify some topic that they would like to investigate, not some topic the teacher wants them to pursue. It is open to and solicits student self-direction and independence. Although familiarizing relating behavior may not be unique for each student, it allows each student to follow his particular interests and, therefore, it is personal. Relating behavior that familiarizes is also humanistic because in a certain sense it is facilitating. It facilitates by helping students to find interesting problems for study. Hopefully, this type of relating behavior will also be genuine, but genuineness is not an inherent quality of familiarizing.

Relating behavior that facilitates student inquiry or problem-solving endeavor is any type of relating behavior that helps students answer the questions they have raised. It can take any of the previously mentioned forms. The teacher can be a source of data himself or he can direct students to sources of data. Relating behavior that facilitates is a behavior that is employed in relation to students' needs. After the student has identified an intriguing problem for himself, the teacher does not, as a matter of course, help the student solve it or solve it for the student. Facts, analyses, and suggestions are only given when and if the student experiences difficulty in comprehending some point or has encountered other problems that may result in unproductive inquiry, and they are only given after the teacher has established that the student has exhausted many other sources of information and is truly in need of aid.

The reason why this kind of relating behavior is humanistic is that it does what its title indicates. It facilitates. It aids student thinking and valuing. It encourages and develops self-direction and independence by helping students overcome discouraging roadblocks in solving their problems and achieving some progress. Relating behavior that facilitates is also receptive and personal. It can take any direction and can be in any form that will be of service to a student. Because most students will be pursuing their own individual problems and the help that is given will vary in kind and quantity from student to student, it is personal.

To get a clearer understanding of what is meant by these two types of humanistic relating behavior and also what nonhumanistic relating behavior is, the following examples are offered:

1. Automobile expressways are an interesting form of mass transportation in urban areas. From our bus trip yesterday and our examination of a map of our city we can see that we have many miles of expressways. One goes through nearly every section of the city. Ten years ago these highways did not exist. There were no superhighways going through the city on which traffic moved at over 50 miles per hour. It seems as though it would have taken longer to get from place to place, not only for passenger cars but also for trucks, buses, and other vehicles. People who were just passing through the city probably spent more time doing it. These expressways are not free, however. They cost millions of dollars to construct and I suspect maintenance is a big problem. I wonder if they are also expensive in terms of increased traffic accidents. And what about pollution? I wonder if they cause more pollution than regular streets? We have all heard about the families that had to find new homes because of expressway construction; that's another expense. Expressways are certainly a worldwide phenomenon of the 1960's and 70's. The many and complex relationships between expressways and the character and quality of human life raise many interesting questions.

2. You have implied that man will never travel to other planets. Perhaps, but have you considered this? The first form of mechanical power used for transportation was the steam engine. Trains were first used in the 1820's. Gasoline engine automobiles were developed in the 1900's. In the 1950's jet engine airplane transportation began. Moon space travel with rocket engines began only two years ago. The whole history of machine transportation spans only 150 years. I wonder what the next 150 years will bring.

3. I noticed, Jim, that you've been having trouble in your investigation of pollution. Remember that there are many types of pollution and many kinds of polluters. There is air pollution, land pollution, and water pollution. It can be done by individuals or by groups, such as governments, factories, and schools. To get a better understanding of the total pollution problem as background for your particular problem of pollution cures that sixth graders can use, I suggest you read these four booklets.

Of these three examples the first is an example of relating behavior that familiarizes. It is an abbreviated example. Actual familiarizing relating behavior would be more lengthy and provide more information about expressways in an effort to touch on enough areas to arouse every student's interest. The other two examples are of relating behavior that facilitates. Both would be issued following problem identification by students. The first of these two presents what might be called an analysis of a student's statement while the second presents relevant facts and suggests a future course of action for a student.

These three are examples of humanistic relating because they familiarize and facilitate. If the purpose had been to inculcate, they would be examples of nonhumanistic behavior. Had it been the teacher's intention to have students take in and remember each of the facts about expressways or to commit for future recall the dates related to machine transportation, the relating behavior would have been far from humanistic.

Before turning to soliciting behavior, one last point concerning relating behavior needs to be made. Besides attention to the purpose of the relating behavior for relating to be humanistic, one must also be concerned with the quantity of relating. Certainly spending from 25 to 50 per cent of classroom time on relating is too much, even if it is familiarizing and facilitating. Inculcating relating behavior needs to be decreased if not eliminated, but extensive familiarizing and facilitating is not wise either. Too much familiarizing and facilitating precludes independent inquiry by students and does not result in a humanistic situation.

Soliciting Behavior

Soliciting like informing is an indispensable tool of the teacher. It is a behavior that demands a verbal or physical response on the part of students. Solicitations are primarily questions, but they can also be commands and requests. During the course of instruction teachers typically use a great number of solicitations. Some of these initiate or begin the treatment of certain topics while others develop or extend discussion of various topics. The term soliciting as used here refers to initiating solicitations. The subject of extending solicitations is dealt with in the section on reacting behaviors.

One way to conceptualize solicitations is from the standpoint of the type of thinking or logical operations required on the part of the respondents. Many researchers interested in teacher questions have studied solicitations from this perspective. An examination of several of these research efforts is useful in identifying humanistic soliciting behavior.

Gallagher working wtih Aschner and others developed an analysis system for examining the quality of thinking expressed in the oral behavior of teachers and students.[16] The system did not deal solely with teacher questions, but teacher questioning or soliciting and its relationship to student answers were an important segment of the study. The system consists of four major categories of thought. The categories with examples are:

1. Cognitive memory thinking

    Cognitive memory thinking operations represent the reproduction of facts or other remembered content, e.g., "Who was the first European to explore the Great Lakes?"

2. Convergent thinking

    Convergent thinking operations involve analysis and integration of data. This operation leads to one expected outcome, e.g., "Why did Great Britain grant independence to so many of its colonies after World War II?"

3. Evaluative thinking

    Evaluative thinking operations involve value judgments, e.g., "Who has been the best President in the last twenty-five years?"

4. Divergent thinking

    Divergent thinking operations call for the generation of fresh, new ideas or directions, e.g., "What changes might occur if the next President were a woman?"

Gallagher's four categories are very similar to the system developed by Davis and Tinsley.[17] In an attempt to determine the types of objectives found in secondary school student teachers' social studies classes as revealed by the questions of the teacher and students, Davis and Tinsley drew heavily on Bloom's *Taxonomy of Educational Objectives; Handbook I: Cognitive Domain*[18] and Sanders' formulations.[19] The instrument that emerged for classifying questions contains eight substantive categories. The categories and examples of them are:

1. Memory

    Memory questions request the recall or recognition of information, e.g., "How frequently does the earth rotate?"

2. Translation

    Translation questions request that information be changed into a different form, e.g., "In your own words, what does the last paragraph of our story mean?"

3. Interpretation

   Interpretation questions request that relationships between various types of data be stated, e.g., "Is Germany a larger or smaller exporter than Japan?"

4. Application

   Application questions request that a realistic problem be solved by using appropriate knowledge and skills, e.g., "Does our city have an adequate pollution control program?"

5. Analysis

   Analysis questions request the solution to a problem in the light of conscious knowledge of the parts and processes of reasoning, e.g., "Tell why the reasoning in the following quotation is sound or unsound: 'Research shows that many kinds of animals are becoming extinct except for some that are preserved in zoos. What we ought to do is capture the remaining wild animals of those species that are becoming extinct and insure their continued existence by placing them in zoos.'"

6. Synthesis

   Synthesis questions request that an original, speculative, or creative problem be answered, e.g., "Should we have a relief program for unemployed persons?"

7. Evaluation

   Evaluation questions request judgments according to explicit criteria, e.g., "Is the migration to suburbs a good thing?"

8. Affectivity

   Affectivity questions request statements of feeling or emotion, e.g., "Do you like Mrs. North?"

Questions or the opening phases of episodes are also examined in the study by Smith and Meux mentioned earlier in relation to relating behavior.[20] To review, these researchers were concerned with the logical operations of teaching—those teacher behaviors that can be evaluated logically by reference to rules of validity and correctness. They chose to focus on the opening phase of episodes because this opening or question controlled the other two phases of the episode: the continuing phase and the closing phase. The categories of logical operations or the kinds of questions that Smith and Meux identify with accompanying examples are the following:

1. Defining

    Defining operations call for the meaning of a term, e.g., "What does terrestrial mean?"

2. Describing

    Describing operations call for an account of something, e.g., "Tell me about the council meeting."

3. Designating

    Designating operations call for the name of an object, e.g., "What do we call a body of land that is surrounded by water on three sides?"

4. Stating

    Stating operations call for statements of issue, conclusions, beliefs, rules, ideas, e.g., "What is the conclusion?"

5. Reporting

    Reporting operations call for a report of information found in a book or document, e.g., "What did you find out about it in the encyclopedia?"

6. Substituting

    Substituting operations call for a symbolic operation usually of a mathematical nature, e.g., "Solve the equation by giving X a value of 5 and Y a value of 8."

7. Evaluating

    Evaluating operations call for estimates of value, worth, and dependability, e.g., "Is the person who wastes drinking water a good citizen?"

8. Opining

    Opining operations are similar to evaluating except that the evidence from which the conclusion is to be drawn is not given, e.g., "Do you think historians will say that the money spent to send men to the moon was well spent?"

9. Classifying

    Classifying operations call for placing given instances into classes to which they belong, e.g., "What type of animal is a sponge?"

10. Comparing and contrasting

    Comparing and contrasting operations call for the comparison of two or more things, e.g., "What is the difference between sleet and hail?"

11. Conditional inferring

   Conditional inferring operations present an antecedent and call for a consequent, e.g., "What is the effect of the country's equatorial location?"

12. Explaining

   Explaining operations present a consequent and call for an antecedent, e.g., "What caused man to create and use tools?"

With these three investigations of solicitations as background, the question of what soliciting behavior is humanistic and what is nonhumanistic can be addressed. Of the kinds of solicitations described above those that are humanistic are divergent, evaluative, synthesis, affectivity, opining, and to a slightly lesser extent convergent, application, analysis, comparing and contrasting, conditional inferring, and explaining. These types of solicitations are humanistic behaviors because they accept and facilitate those human qualities that each student possesses: thinking and valuing. Divergent and synthesis questions permit rational thought of the highest order, while evaluating, opining, and affectivity solicitations allow students to express their feelings and values. Analysis, convergent, inferring, and explaining behaviors also develop critical thinking abilities. Further, these types of solicitations are humanistic because they give students freedom to develop self-direction. Questions that call for divergence or evaluation are completely open questions; there are infinite acceptable responses the student could give to questions such as these. What he is required to do is decide for himself which answer or answers of the many he could give are the most appropriate. He must exercise his independence when confronted with such questions. The great freedom of response that these kinds of questions permit make them personal behaviors. Each individual student can respond to them in a unique way.

The types of solicitation that are nonhumanistic are the remaining types: cognitive-memory, translation, interpretation, defining, describing, designating, stating, reporting, and substituting. Questions such as these restrict and inhibit thinking and valuing. They, in effect, say to the student, "You are not capable of independent, rational thought or making judgments for yourself. What you are capable of is remembering and doing what you are told." Memory, describing, translation, and the others call for little thought and almost no self-direction. For each one of these questions there is but one or a very limited number of correct responses.

The research findings that exist illustrate quite clearly that the kinds of solicitations used most frequently are of the nonhumanistic variety.

In studying productive thought with academically talented students at the junior high school level Gallagher found that cognitive-memory and convergent thinking occurred the most frequently, and divergent and evaluative thinking rarely. This finding concerns total classroom behavior but is most certainly true for questions. Davis and Tinsley found that the questions that received repeated use in secondary social studies classes were memory and interpretation. The secondary teachers in many subject areas of Smith and Meux's study used primarily describing and designating solicitations, but also used explaining solicitation quite frequently.

Solicitations that call for independent thinking and valuing are an important aspect of creating a humanistic teaching-learning encounter. Solicitations that cause dependence and restrict thinking and valuing if used exclusively or mainly, as research seems to indicate, destroy humanism. There are times when the use of these restricting solicitations may be necessary. It may be essential to determine if a student remembers a particular fact or event, or to set the context for posing thinking and valuing questions, one may need to ask a few recall or interpretation questions. If a humanistic situation is to exist, the majority of initiating solicitations must be those that permit thinking and valuing. But even the quantity of these kinds of solicitations in relation to other teacher behaviors and to other student behaviors cannot be large. If the teacher uses too many initiating solicitations, there will be little time for the development of the student's response, student solicitations, and student reacting, and, consequently, humanism will not be served.

In an effort to further clarify humanistic soliciting behavior, the initiating solicitations from a brief lesson on credit cards at the fourth-grade level were abstracted. These solicitations are:

1. What is a credit card, Peter?
2. What is a credit card good for? Why have them?
3. What types of credit cards are there?
4. Are credit cards a convenience? Are they a good thing?
5. Should all people have credit cards? What do you think? Alice?
6. What would be the result or effect of not having credit, if credit cards didn't exist?
7. What about credit of the future? How might credit be handled in 2001?

Of these seven questions, the first three are nonhumanistic. They may serve the function of "warming up" the class or setting the stage for thinking, but they require only minimal thinking and are restrictive. They all call for memory of some kind. The first requests a definition while two and three require stating and describing. The other four questions are humanistic behaviors. They are open, permissive questions that encourage considerable rational thought and valuing. Question four is an evaluative question; questions five and seven are synthesis or divergent thinking questions; and question six is a convergent or conditional inferring question. With several additional questions like the last four and perhaps with the replacement of one or more of the first three "warm-up" questions with thought or value questions, this lesson could very well have been a humanistic experience for students. To determine if it actually was a humanistic class session, however, we need to know what informing, responding, and reacting were also occurring. Responding is the next behavior that is examined.

Responding Behavior[21]

Responding behavior refers to the answering of students' questions or in any way fulfilling the expectation of students' solicitations. Responding, in contrast to informing and soliciting, is a reflexive behavior. Reacting is a reflexive behavior too. Because responding and reacting are reflexive they have greater potential for developing humanistic situations than do informing and soliciting. Informing and soliciting indicate how receptive, facilitating, personal, and hopefully genuine the teacher *intends* to be. How the teacher responds to student questions or reacts to student responses shows how open and ready to serve the teacher really is. One can use very general structuring or ask divergent questions, but how the teacher responds and reacts to student behavior is indicative of just how much self-direction and thought students are permitted.

The responding behavior of teachers is *terra incognita*. There is a paucity of information about responding probably because the person who usually responds in classroom interaction is not the teacher, but the student. According to Bellack's study 5.5 per cent of teacher behaviors are responding while 65.4 per cent of student behaviors are responding. Or, to view it another way, of all the responding behavior that occurs, 12.0 per cent of it is performed by teachers and 88.0 per cent by students. If humanism is to be served, students need to decrease their responding behavior and increase their solicitation behavior, while teachers need to do just the converse. Suggestions on how to increase student questioning are given in Chapter 3.

Assuming that students ask many questions in classrooms, how should teachers respond to them in an effort to develop the important human qualities that students possess? The behaviors that many teachers use in response to student solicitations are inadequate if not harmful. Some typical kinds of responses to student questions and examples of each are:

1. Put off substantive questions not directly related to the content under consideration, e.g., "We'll be studying that next spring when we get to electricity, Jim."
2. Provide simple answers to complex and particularly intriguing questions related to the content, e.g., "The reason why Hitler hated Jews was because he spent his formative years in Vienna where a great deal of anti-Semitism existed at the time."
3. Admonish students to find their own answers to reproduction or recall questions, e.g., "Look up the spelling in your dictionary."
4. Refuse to repeat answers to procedural questions, e.g., "I'm sorry, John, but I've told you before when the project is due."

Responses such as these are not humanistic behaviors. In the first example the teacher is unreceptive to a student's interest. He dismisses an opportunity to develop thought and self-direction. In the second example the teacher destroys independent inquiry that could easily have been nurtured. By this behavior he terminates rather than facilitates student thought. In the third example it appears that the teacher is helping a student to be self-directed but he may be discouraging it by causing the student to interrupt his investigation of a significant problem with that which presents unimportant details. Depending on the context in which it is used, the fourth example could be humanistic, but it probably is not for the same reason applicable to the third example.

Of these four kinds of teacher responses, the second is a direct answer and the others are indirect answers. The second meets the request of the student. The others do not. When to respond to student questions with direct answers and when and how to respond to student questions with indirect answers is what makes the response humanistic or nonhumanistic.

Direct, straightforward responses to students' questions are humanistic behaviors when the student needs the answer to the question he has asked in order to achieve a larger and more important objective he is pursuing. Requests for spellings, word pronunciation, specific substantive facts, verification of observations, repeat of directions, and other requests dealing with memory and procedure should be met if they are incurred while the student is en route to the solution of a problem. Direct responses in situations like these facilitate inquiry and are probably always personal because they are usually given to one student in relation to his needs or interests rather than to many. They increase self-direction and responsibility by eliminating or reducing minor distractions of having to look up a forgotten fact or the plural form of a word so that all of the student's energy can be devoted to attempting to solve more important substantive problems on his own. Direct, straightforward responses are also humanistic when the student's question has little or no inquiry potential but is a high-level, sincere, and honest question in which the student is interested, or when the question calls for development of a previous response. Direct responses in these situations certainly contribute to rational thought of students and demonstrate the teacher's genuineness. If a teacher made the following responses to student questions he would be displaying humanistic behavior:

1. Student: Mr. Arnold, I'm just finishing my letter to Alderman Tanzivsky about trash collection information and I've forgotten how to spell "municipal."
   Teacher: M-u-n-i-c-i-p-a-l.
2. Student: I'm now comparing exports of the two countries, but the information is given in British pounds. How much is a pound worth in our money?
   Teacher: Two dollars and forty cents.
3. Student: I think that this plant is slightly greener than this one, don't you?
   Teacher: It looks to me like it is, Tina.
4. Student: What are your feelings about the story, Miss Knapp?
   Teacher: I loved it. It reminded me of my childhood in California.

Indirect responses, responses that are not given in a straightforward manner, should be given when the student's solicitation is one that (1) calls for productive thought or valuations, (2) deals with content that is of significance to the student, and (3) has the potential for engaging the student in inquiry for an extended period of time. Solicitations of students that should be answered in an indirect way if they meet these three criteria are what Gallagher terms convergent, divergent, and evaluative thinking questions, or what Smith and Meux call application, analysis, synthesis, and opining questions. Examples of these types of questions in addition to those mentioned in the preceding section are:

1. Why did the pilgrims wear such dark clothing?
2. Will man ever travel to Venus?
3. Why isn't the capital of Wisconsin in Milwaukee rather than Madison?

4. Why don't poor people end their lazy habits and get jobs?
5. Why do we have a county government *and* a city government?
6. Why are old people so narrow-minded?
7. Had President Kennedy lived, would he have supported a heavy U. S. involvement in Vietnam?

When student solicitations like these are heard by the teacher, the teacher should immediately "count-to-ten" in an effort to resist a desire to answer them directly and to plan how he will respond to them indirectly.

Questions such as these which have great inquiry possibilities should be answered with statements or with other questions that cause the student to think about his question or problem and how he might solve it. First of all the teacher should help the student clarify his question—what it means, what it includes, what it assumes, what its antecedents are. After the question is clarified, the teacher's next task is to help the student identify a plan of attack. His responses would then deal with where, how, and when to collect data.

Indirect responding behavior that clarifies and develops is often indistinguishable from one kind of teacher humanistic reacting behavior which is explored in depth in the following section. Some examples of this behavior are given here. Additional examples and greater discussion of clarifying and developing are present there. Three examples are:

1. Student solicitation: Miss Kanger, why do firemen wear such funny hats?
   Teacher response: Which hats do you mean, Terry? Why do you say they're funny?
2. Student solicitation: Why do some seeds sprout faster than others even when they are planted at the same time?
   Teacher response: How did you come to that conclusion? What exactly did you do and what happened?
3. Student solicitation: I know I've got to interview consumers to find out the effects of the increased sales tax, but how else can I get information?
   Teacher response: Well, perhaps you need to think on a broader scale, to consider the complete production-consumption process.

These behaviors are obviously receptive, facilitating, and personal. Growth in independent thinking, valuing, and acting are seemingly natural consequences of such behavior.

TEACHER BEHAVIOR

Reacting Behavior

Behavior that rates and judges student comments or actions or that attempts to develop or change it in some way is teacher reacting behavior. Most typically teacher reacting behavior occurs following a student response to a teacher solicitation. The positive and negative judgments that teachers often make after student responses are reacting behavior, as are the comments and questions urging students to support their ideas or to elaborate on them. This behavior along with teacher responding is of special importance in creating humanistic encounters because of the power it has in controlling or influencing student behavior.

Reacting behavior of teachers has been studied by several investigators. Here, as in the preceding sections, a brief survey of concepts from these studies provides a perspective for discussing specific humanistic behavior, in this case humanistic reacting.

Zahorik studied the rating aspect of the reacting move.[22] He was interested in the feedback reacting behavior provides for students. What teachers say or do following student behavior can provide information to the student about the value of his behavior. Theoretically, this feedback information can help students adjust and control their subsequent behavior. To determine the kinds of feedback or ratings teachers use and to what extent they use each kind, a feedback system consisting of 25 categories was developed. Some of these categories with examples are the following:

1. Simple praise-confirmation

    Common words or short phrases that provide limited praise or confirmation, e.g., "Good," "All right."

2. Elaborate praise

    Unusual words or phrases that provide more extensive praise than simple praise-confirmation, e.g., "That's excellent thinking, Tom." "Wonderful!"

3. Simple reproof-denial

    Common words or short phrases that give limited reproof or denial, e.g., "No," "Un uh."

4. Elaborate reproof

    Unusual words or phrases that give more extensive reproof than simple reproof-denial, e.g., "You aren't using your head."

5. Praise-confirmation and reproof-denial

   Remarks that indicate that a student's behavior is partially acceptable or unacceptable, or that it may be acceptable or unacceptable but no decision is being made for the present, e.g., "Yes and no," "Maybe."

6. Positive answer repetition

   Positive answer refers to remarks that repeat, paraphrase, or summarize students' acceptable behavior, e.g., "Africa." (After student responds with "Africa" to a question concerning the location of Nigeria).

7. Negative answer repetition

   This behavior refers to remarks that repeat, paraphrase, or summarize students' unacceptable behavior, e.g., "Europe?" (After student responds with "Europe" to a question concerning the location of Nigeria.)

8. Positive explanation

   Remarks that provide reasons why a student's behavior is acceptable, e.g., "Thailand is correct because the 'h' is silent." (After student responds with "Tiland" to question concerning the pronunciation of Thailand.)

9. Negative explanation

   Remarks that provide reasons why a student's behavior is unacceptable, e.g., ". . . the 'h' is silent and so is the 'a.'" (After student responds with "Thaland" to question concerning the pronunciation of Thailand.)

These categories represent direct feedback or rating. They communicate the teacher's judgment about the student's remarks or actions in a direct manner. The instrument also contains categories that deal with indirect feedback. Teachers rate students indirectly when they decide to develop a response, or repeat a previous solicitation, or launch a new initiating solicitation. Since these behaviors are analyzed from other perspectives elsewhere in the chapter they are not dealt with here.

In a study concerning the thinking of elementary school students Taba and Elzey deal with the development or modification aspect of reacting behavior.[23] They developed a multidimensional instrument which permitted them to examine the relationship between teaching functions and levels of thought. Some of the functions they identified which are or can be developing or modifying reacting behavior and examples of each are:

1. Controlling thought
   Controlling thought refers to the performing of cognitive tasks by the teacher that students ought to be performing, such as giving a category for classification, e.g., "That would be a vegetable, too." (After student responds with "lettuce" to teacher question concerning types of plants.)
2. Extending thought
   Extending thought refers to the giving or seeking of additional information, elaboration, or clarification of a topic, e.g., "Tell me more about that, Mike."
3. Lifting thought
   Lifting thought refers to the giving or seeking of thinking on a level above that which is being engaged in, such as from concept formation to the induction of generalizations, e.g., "Explain why."

The development or modification aspect of reacting is also dealt with in another study by Zahorik.[24] In this study the relationship of planning to teaching was investigated. The effects of preplanning on teaching were compared with those of nonplanning. One of the teacher behaviors that was examined was data extenders. This behavior refers to teacher statements or solicitations that deal with the preceding student's remarks. Two types of data extenders were studied:

1. Nonauthentic data extenders
   This behavior refers to comments that provide or request only limited or no extension of student behavior. Summarizing student responses, restating the original solicitation, introducing clues leading to an answer to the original solicitation, and shaping a student's ideas so that the teacher's ideas emerge are nonauthentic data extenders. Examples are: "So, you have been saying that credit cards are useful if you don't want to carry large sums of cash or if you don't have cash at the moment; What's another type of credit card, Tom?" (After another student gives one type of credit card.)
2. Authentic data extenders
   Authentic data extenders are comments that provide or request extension of student behavior. Types of authentic data extenders are asking a student to expand his or another pupil's point, giving expansion of a student's thinking and reflecting a student's comment to determine if he communicated the meaning he intended.

Examples are: "Why do you feel that not everybody should be able to have a credit card?" (After student indicates that not everyone should have a credit card); "Tell us more about entertainment credit cards." (After student states that his father pays hotel bills with an entertainment credit card.)

Authentic data extenders are very similar to Taba and Elzey's extension and lifts and also to what Raths terms the value clarifying response.[25] Raths, in relation to his concern for the apparent lack of values in students and the difficulty in acquiring values today, developed several procedures that teachers could use to help students acquire values. One of these procedures is the value clarifying response. It is a developing reacting behavior that is used following student comments that deal with attitudes, aspirations, activities, or purposes. Raths calls these value related areas value indicators, and it is the function of the value clarifying response to raise value indicators to the level of values. For a value indicator to become a value it must meet seven criteria. The seven criteria and examples of clarifying responses that teachers might use in an effort to help students meet the criteria and develop values are:

1. Choosing freely
   "Where did you get that idea?"
2. Choosing from alternatives
   "What did you consider before making your decision?"
3. Choosing thoughtfully and reflectively
   "What will be the result of this action?"
4. Prizing and cherishing
   "Are you happy about your plan?"
5. Affirming
   "Would you be willing to present your idea to the other members?"
6. Acting upon choices
   "Has this feeling affected your life?"
7. Repeating
   "Would you do that again or not?"

With this background concerning reacting behavior we can now turn to the question of what is humanistic reacting behavior and what is non-humanistic reacting behavior.

For reacting to be humanistic, there must be decreased use of rating. Most reacting is rating, even the casual observer of teaching would conclude. Bellack's results show that the reacting behavior of his secondary school teachers was to a great extent some type of rating. Zahorik's study on feedback shows that the rating that occurs is mostly perfunctory. What teachers appear to do most frequently following student remarks is to repeat them approvingly or mildly praise and confirm them and then issue a new initiating solicitation. Other findings concerning the value of feedback show that these perfunctory types of rating do not provide a great deal of cognitive information nor are they particularly reinforcing or motivational.

If these simple rating behaviors are not effective in promoting student learning, that is justification to question their continued extensive use, but from a humanistic orientation their use should be decreased for other reasons. It should be decreased because when teachers are rating they are often not developing or clarifying. Although it is possible to rate and develop at the same time, usually rating ends the treatment of a topic or idea. If rating is used without accompanying development reacting it discourages and restricts rather than encourages and facilitates students' thinking and valuing, even if it is a form of praise or confirmation. An "O.K." or "Good" signals that a topic will not be pursued any further, and that the slate is now clean for new action, just as a "no" or "Un uh" does.

Further, extensive perfunctory rating is nonhumanistic because it makes students dependent on the teacher. If teachers use perfunctory rating incessantly students come to expect it and tend not to act until a preceding act has been duly approved.

Constant and frequent use of rating is nonhumanistic, but there are times when its use is necessary and advisable. One of those times is to encourage student humanistic behavior when students first begin to display it. When students first begin to venture on their own, to take independent stands on issues, to show responsibility, to uncover topics with inquiry potential, to express their values, or in any other way to be the unique rational and feeling persons that they are, teachers ought to react with strong encouragement. In situations like these, elaborate praise with explanations concerning why the student's behavior is praiseworthy is appropriate and facilitating. Elaborate praise and explanations should be used because they provide substantial feedback value, they are usually individual, personal statements rather than stereotyped statements, and since they provide reasons they recognize and enhance students' rationality.

After students begin to display humanistic behaviors regularly, elaborate praise with accompanying explanations can be reduced. From a humanistic point of view it is essential that students' ideas, feelings, and interests be continuously encouraged, but this can be done in other more humanistic ways. It can be done through development and modification reacting. What could be more receptive and encouraging than to have the teacher actually deal with a student's idea, not to dismiss it by rating it perfunctorily, but to delve into it by clarifying it, extending it, or lifting it?

In addition to decreasing rating for reacting behavior to be humanistic, there must be vastly increased development or modification reacting behavior. There needs to be constant probing, clarifying, and justifying of students' behavior. The particular behaviors that perform this function are extensions or authentic data extenders, lifts, and value clarifying responses. These behaviors are humanistic because of the great power they have in communicating to students the acceptance and worth of their ideas, feelings, and actions and in facilitating rational thought and clarification of values. Through development and modification reacting behavior of these types students' independent thinking ability and valuing capacity are recognized, exercised, and advanced. They are also humanistic because they usually are personal; they are usually directed at one student rather than many.

Not all development or modification reacting behavior is humanistic, however. Controlling thought and nonauthentic data extenders are nonhumanistic teacher behaviors. They are contrary to the goals of humanistic teacher behavior.

The following are examples of humanistic reacting behavior:

1. Teacher solicitation: What interests you the most about Antarctica?
   Student response: One of the things I'm really interested in is the fact that nobody lives there, except maybe some scientists. Eskimos live at the North Pole, but there are no native people of the South Pole. This really interests me.
   Teacher reaction: I never thought of that, Jack. That's really an exciting thought! It's got tremendous research possibilities.
2. Teacher solicitation: What do you think is the future of the downtown areas of large cities?
   Student response: I think they'll look like they did a long time ago.
   Teacher reaction: What do you mean by that? Could you tell us more, Peggy?

3. Teacher solicitation: Do you agree that the term of office for the President should be a four-year term?
Student response: The term of office should be eight to ten years.
Teacher reaction: Why? What are your reasons for advocating a longer term?
4. Teacher solicitation: In Tuesday's election only 18.3 per cent of the eligible voters voted. Shouldn't everybody vote?
Student response: I think only certain people should vote. I think only smart people, college graduates, should be allowed to vote and run the country.
Teacher reaction: How long have you felt this way, Michael?

The first example is elaborate praise with explanation. The student has uncovered a particularly intriguing problem that has considerable inquiry potential. The teacher tells him in a direct way that his thought is indeed a good one, and why it is a good one. In the second example the teacher is extending the pupil's remarks. Rather than moving on to other students' responses to the initiating solicitation, the teacher calls for elaboration and clarification. Example three is lifting reaction. The teacher requests explanation and justification of the student's response. He is going to explore the student's idea in greater depth. The last example is of value clarification. The student has expressed a value indicator and the teacher is attempting to get the student to think about his position, to reflect on whether or not his decision was made freely.

The examination of humanistic reacting behavior completes the discussion of humanistic teacher behavior. It was the intent of this chapter to present and analyze specific teacher informing, soliciting, responding, and reacting behaviors that are consistent with the goals and criteria of humanistic teaching. All of the specific humanistic teacher behaviors that were identified and explored were shown to compare favorably with the criteria of humanistic teaching. Most often the behaviors were only shown to be receptive, facilitating, and personal. The criterion of genuineness was frequently overlooked, but not because of lack of importance. Genuineness is a most important quality of humanistic teacher behavior. It is a quality, however, that is difficult to illustrate. It is more of a pervading attitude than a characteristic that teachers must have if the goals of humanistic instruction are to be achieved. If this criterion is not met, it is immaterial if the other criteria are met.

In the following chapter humanistic student behavior using the same model of instruction is discussed.

Notes

1. James B. Macdonald, "The High School in Human Terms: Curriculum Design." *Humanizing the Secondary School,* ed. Norman K. Hamilton and J. Galen Saylor (Washington, D. C.: Associate for Supervision and Curriculum Development, 1969), p. 51.
2. Dwayne Huebner, "Moral Values and the Curriculum." (Paper read at Conference on Moral Dilemmas of Schooling, Madison, Wisconsin: University of Wisconsin, 1965.)
3. Carl R. Rogers, "The Facilitation of Significant Learning." *Instruction: Some Contemporary Viewpoints,* ed. Laurence Siegel (San Francisco: Chandler Publishing Company, 1967), pp. 43-46.
4. Macdonald, *loc. cit.*
5. Earl C. Kelley, "The Fully Functioning Self." *Perceiving, Behaving, Becoming.* Yearbook 1962 of the Association for Supervision and Curriculum Development, (Washington, D. C.: The Association, 1962), pp. 9-20.
6. Carl R. Rogers, "Toward Becoming a Fully Functioning Person." *Perceiving, Behaving, Becoming.* Yearbook 1962 of the Association for Supervision and Curriculum Development, (Washington, D. C.: The Association, 1962), pp. 21-33.
7. Arno A. Bellack, *et al., The Language of the Classroom* (New York: Teachers College Press, 1966).
8. Bellack, *op. cit.*
9. Marie M. Hughes and Associates. *The Assessment of the Quality of Teaching: A Research Report,* U. S. Office of Education, Cooperative Research Project No. 353, (Salt Lake City: University of Utah, 1959).
10. Hilda Taba, Samuel Levine, and Freeman F. Elzey, *Thinking in Elementary School Children.* U. S. Office of Education, Cooperative Research Project, No. 1574, (San Francisco: San Francisco State College, 1964).
11. B. Othanel Smith, and Milton O. Meux with others. *A Study of the Logic of Teaching.* U. S. Office of Education, Cooperative Research Project, No. 258, (Urbana: University of Illinois, 1960).
12. Edmund Amidon, and Elizabeth Hunter. *Improving Teaching* (New York: Holt, Rinehart & Winston, Inc., 1966).
13. Ned A. Flanders, *Teacher Influence, Pupil Attitudes, and Achievement.* U. S. Office of Education, Cooperative Research Project No. 397, (Minneapolis: University of Minnesota, 1960).
14. M. Vere DeVault, Dan W. Anderson, and John Withall (eds.) *Insights Into Mental Health and Teacher Education.* National Institute of Mental Health, Grant 2M-6624, (Madison, Wisconsin: University of Wisconsin, 1966).
15. Wilbert W. Lewis, J. M. Newall, and John Withall. "An Analysis of Classroom Patterns of Communication," *Psychological Report,* IX (1961), pp. 211-219.
16. James J. Gallagher, *Productive Thinking of Gifted Children.* U. S. Office of Education, Cooperative Research Project, No. 965, (Urbana: University of Illinois, 1965).
17. O. L. Davis, Jr., and Drew O. Tinsely. "Cognitive Objectives Revealed by Classroom Questions Asked by Social Studies Student Teachers," *Peabody Journal of Education,* LXV (July, 1967), pp. 21-26.

18. Benjamin S. Bloom, (ed.). *Taxonomy of Educational Objectives; Handbook I: Cognitive Domain*, (New York: David McKay Co., Inc., 1956).

19. Norris M. Sanders, *Classroom Questions: What Kinds?* (New York: Harper and Row, 1966).

20. Smith, *op. cit.*

21. Several of the ideas contained in this section are found in the following publication, but they are used here in a different context:
John A. Zahorik, "Questioning in the Classroom," *Education*. XCIX (April-May, 1971), pp. 358-363.

22. John A. Zahorik, "Classroom Feedback Behavior of Teachers," *Journal of Educational Research*, LXII (December, 1968), pp. 147-150; John A. Zahorik, "Pupils' Perceptions of Teachers' Verbal Feedback," *The Elementary School Journal*. LXXI (November, 1970), pp. 105-114.

23. Taba, *op. cit.*

24. John A. Zahorik, "The Effect of Planning on Teaching," *The Elementary School Journal*, LXXI (December, 1970), pp. 143-151.

25. Louis E. Raths, Merrill Harmin, and Sidney B. Simon. *Values and Teaching: Working with Values in the Classrooms* (Columbus, Ohio: Charles E. Merrill Books, Inc. 1966).

Student Behavior

Identifying and discussing humanistic teacher behavior is only half of the task of providing a specific, detailed description of humanistic behavior. To complete the description, student classroom behavior that is humanistic must also be identified and examined. Student behavior that would be considered humanistic was indirectly indicated to a certain extent in the preceding chapter. It was dealt with as the product of humanistic teacher behavior. The purpose of this chapter is to focus directly on the student and present and explore those behaviors of the student that are humanistic.

Student classroom behavior may be termed humanistic if it consists of the human qualities that each student possesses. Although these qualities have been identified and referred to in Chapter 2, a restatement and elaboration of them is a prerequisite to an analysis of humanistic classroom behavior of students.

The humanistic qualities that each student or each man possesses are the capacity for self-direction, independence, and responsibility, and for thinking, valuing, feeling, and creating. The extent to which the student realizes this capacity and displays these qualities is the extent to which he is a humanistic person.

Self-direction, independence, and responsibility refer to the student's ability to be his own man, to decide for himself, to act on his convictions, to be accountable for his beliefs and actions. It means to not follow others or submit to authority blindly, but to challenge the accepted and the sacred when they are in conflict with one's intuitions, even when the challenger is a minority of one. The thoroughly human person will resist efforts to be dominated. He will insist on independent choice and accept the consequences it will bring. To settle for less reduces one's humanness. Dostoevsky reflects this view when he says, "What man wants is simply independent choice, whatever that independence may cost and wherever it may lead."[1] Perhaps the total quality of self-direction, independence, and responsibility is best expressed by Thoreau:

If a man does not keep pace with his companions, perhaps it is because he hears a different drummer. Let him step to the music that he hears, however measured or far away. It is not important that he matures as an apple tree or an oak. Shall he turn his spring into summer?[2]

The quality of thinking refers to the ability to solve problems, to inquire, to employ logical argument. It includes the capacity to compare and contrast, uncover assumptions, summarize, classify, explain, observe, criticize, imagine, hypothesize, synthesize, apply principles, organize data, make decisions, evaluate, and infer. In short, it refers to reason, to use reason, and to be reasoned with. Reasoning ability or rational thought has long been viewed as the primary quality of humanism. This idea has as much validity today as when Socrates and his disciplines expressed it. The student who is not a reasoning person, who is unperceptive, is not curious, does not seek to understand, accepts dictum, or cannot persevere on a problem is not achieving his human potential.

The human quality of valuing means the process of formulating ideals or goals that give direction to life, that serve as a guide to consistent behavior. Valuing, according to Raths, consists of choosing, prizing, and acting.[3] If one chooses from alternatives and with reflection, if he is pleased with his choice and tells others about it, and if his choice results in action repeatedly, he is displaying his human capacity for valuing. Accepting, cherishing, and acting on another's values or ideals or beliefs is to violate one's humanity.

Feeling, as a human quality, refers to emotional sensitivity. It refers to the capacity to show love, affection, caring, anger, compassion, empathy, humor, and other inner feelings. A person who inhibits laughing or crying, worrying or joking, venturing or fearing is not humanistic. The humanist enjoys a full measure of life.

The quality of creating refers to the inventing of newness, to the creation of knowledge and understanding of self and the world. If a student is to be a humanistic person he must be a developer of concepts and generalizations, and he must be aware of and make use of the role of words and symbolization in the creation of knowledge. A person who does not create knowledge but accepts it as being certain and impersonal has not reached his human potential.

With this elaboration of human qualities, the discussion can now move to the identification and examination of specific humanistic behavior of students. As a scheme for conceptualizing student behavior, the model consisting of the four elements of informing, soliciting, responding, and reacting is used. Employing the same model for examining both humanistic teacher behavior and humanistic student behavior permits comparisons between actual behaviors and roles in relation to humanistic instruction.

Perhaps the most important change that needs to occur for student classroom behavior to be humanistic is for there to be a role reversal of teachers and pupils. Casual observations of teaching as well as Bellack's findings[4] clearly show that the teacher's typical role in classrooms is to set the stage for learning, give information, ask questions of students, and rate or react to students' answers. The student's role has traditionally been to answer questions. To structure class situations, ask questions of the teacher and other students, and rate or explore the teacher's response or other students' responses are usually not done. Rather than the teacher being the informer, solicitor, and reactor, and the student the responder, the student should, to some extent, act as the informer, solicitor, and reactor, and the teacher likewise as the responder. The plea here is not for a complete role reversal because that would be unrealistic given the present nature and functioning of schools, but for a partial reversal.

As students begin to assume more and more the traditional teacher role and the teacher assumes the role of the students, the student behavior will become more humanistic. When the student's only role or major role is to respond to the teacher's initiating solicitations, then passivity, dependence, and timidity are encouraged. However, when the student's role is to inform, solicit, and react as well as to respond to other students and the teacher, he becomes more active, he is faced with choices and decisions, he gains a measure of control over and responsibility for his own learning. He becomes involved in independent thinking, valuing, feeling, and creating. Specific types and patterns of humanistic student informing, soliciting, responding, and reacting along with examples and explications as to why the behaviors are humanistic, follow. The concepts and research results presented in Chapter 2 to provide background for discussing humanistic teacher behavior in relation to informing, soliciting, responding, and reacting will also be used here, but will not be reexamined in any detail. The reader may benefit from a review of the concepts presented in Chapter 2 before proceeding further.

Informing Behavior

The most important point for student informing behavior to be humanistic behavior is that there must be greater use of informing by students in comparison to that of the teacher. Both structuring and relating, the two subbehaviors of informing, must be behaviors that students are permitted and encouraged to use if the student's total classroom behavior is to be humanistic.

Structuring, to review, refers to setting the context in which teaching and learning will occur. It usually serves to begin classroom activities by indicating what the activity will be, who will be involved in it, what the topic will be, what logical process will be employed, and what materials will be used. Increased student structuring can take several forms: teacher-student cooperative structuring, student self-structuring, and student-student structuring.

Teacher and students involved in structuring cooperatively is an effective action in beginning the role reversal of teachers and students and moving toward more student self-structuring and student-student structuring. We have seen from the previous chapter that teacher structuring which contains a few broad dimensions of the structuring act also encourages student structuring. Teacher-student structuring is behavior in which both the teacher and the students are involved equally in initiating or ending some activity. The activity, participants, time regulations, logical process, and other considerations can come from either the teacher or the students. This form of humanistic structuring can be more closed, that is, it can contain the dimensions of agent, time, regulations, and aids, and the activity, topic, logical process, and other dimensions can be specific, than teacher structuring because the students are participating in the act. They are participating in independent, responsible decision-making. Their views and ideas are already represented in the behavior.

Two examples of teacher-student humanistic structuring are the following:

1. Teacher: What we seem to be saying about what we're going to do for the first hour this morning is that we're going to hold small group discussions to evaluate the role playing activity from yesterday so that we can improve in today's role playing activity.

2. Student: Let's get started then. We all agree that from now until recess our group needs to see the film on Eskimos again and try to make a list of all of the questions that are raised about customs.

Both of these examples launch activity, they indicate time duration—first hour and time until recess, who will be involved in the activity—everyone and one group of students, the activity—group discussion and viewing a film and listing questions, the topic—role playing and Eskimo customs, and the process—evaluate and identify. Also, the first example contains a reason and the second indicates an instructional aid to be used.

Hopefully, teacher-student cooperative structuring will lead to student self-structuring and student-student structuring. In self-structuring the student decides for himself what activity he will engage in, what topic he will pursue, what logical process he will employ, what his time regulations are, and other matters. He is his own organizer, motivator, and programmer. This form of student structuring behavior is intensely humanistic because it requires a great deal of self-directed, responsible thought and action.

Since self-structuring is only for the person who is doing the structuring, it can be quite closed, even more so than teacher-student structuring. All of the dimensions in a specific form can be present. Although self-structuring may not be communicated or actually stated verbally, the following are examples of student self-structuring:

1. Student: Mr. Williams, what I've decided to do for my project on Mexican art today is to read and summarize this book on Mexican mosaics.
2. Student: Now I know what I'm going to do. During language class today I'm going to make a list of all the ways I can think of to begin stories. Then when I write a story, I can just pick the beginning I like the best.

In both of these examples an activity is launched by announcing and the activity, agent, topic, process, and time are given. Further, the first example includes instructional aids and the second includes a reason for the activity.

Student-student structuring refers to the structuring one student may do for one or more other students. Essentially, this is a behavior in which one student helps others to organize and begin an activity. This is, of course, a humanistic act for the student doing the structuring because again he must exercise self-direction and think for himself. However, it is also necessary that the structuring behavior be a humanistic act for the students who are receiving it. For this to occur, the behavior itself must be relatively open. This type of structuring actually substitutes for teacher structuring and, therefore, must meet all of the requirements of humanistic teacher structuring. The elements of the structuring behavior must be few and general as in the following examples:

1. Student: Why don't you guys do this. Why don't you talk about your favorite parts of the film, the ones you thought were the most interesting.

2. Student: I think the problem you kids will be having is the same one I had earlier. The best way to get information about what schools are like in France is to write a letter to one of the addresses that Mrs. Klemp gave us. But that takes so long, and besides it may be written in French. I'm sure you'll find other good ways to get that information.

The first example meets the requirements and so does the second. In the first the activity, topic, and process are quite general, and the time, aids, regulations, and reasons are not present. The second example is a proposition rather than an announcement and contains even fewer elements and is more general than the first.

Relating is the other aspect of informing. Relating refers to substantive statements of fact, inference, explanation, opinion, interpretation and others. It is an initiating behavior. When a student relates he is not responding to a question from his teacher, he is making a substantive statement on his own volition.

Relating as much as structuring is an act that has been reserved for the teacher. It needs, however, to receive increased usage by students. Students need to offer suggestions, relate facts, give explanations, voice opinions, and make inferences on their own. Relating by students is humanistic because it requires the use of and develops human qualities. Creating and sending a substantive message without aid or coercion certainly involves independent and responsible rational thought and inventiveness, and, quite possibly, valuing and feeling.

For teacher relating behavior to be humanistic it had to either acquaint students in an effort to stimulate their interests and help them to raise questions or facilitate students' inquiry after they had identified questions or problems that intrigued them. It was not to have students remember or internalize some particular fact or explanation. These same requirements are not inappropriate for describing humanistic student relating. If the behavior performs an acquaintanceship function for other students or the teacher or if it facilitates inquiry by other students, it is humanistic. However, in relation to student relating, the acquaintanceship function needs to be interpreted more broadly. The student's acquaintanceship behavior may not be as purposeful or deliberate in attempting to stimulate the curiosity of others. Any acquaintanceship behavior that does not seek to inculcate and, therefore, does not restrict freedom and is not an invasion of the person to whom the behavior is directed, is humanistic relating.

Student relating that is humanistic is shown in these examples:

1. Student: I've listened to my mother talk with her friends about antiques, and you know, you can really tell a lot from the

antiques about how people lived in the old days. Lots of the stuff we have is about a hundred years old and I know a lot about Lincoln's time from it. Our moustache cups show that people, men at least, had moustaches. Also, some of our wooden chairs have curved leg pieces that were made especially for hoop skirts. And our clock shows that the people could keep good time, but the clock had to be wound every single day.

2. Student: I think I see what your problem is, Scott. You've been trying to find out what it was like living in this city during the 1920's by reading those textbooks and library books. What I would do, if I were you, is to phone my Grandmother. She could tell lots of stuff about it because I think she's 80 now, and that would make her about 30 during that time.

Of these examples the first familiarizes and the second facilitates. The first example acquaints the total class, students and teacher, with nineteenth-century life in the United States. In it the student does not expect mastery of his thoughts by others. He is merely engaged in a type of "show and tell" that relates to a general area being studied. The second example facilitates the inquiry of another student. One student is helping another resolve a problem that is a temporary roadblock to him. The student receiving the relating behavior has already tried to solve his problem in several ways. Had the one student helped the other before help was really needed, the behavior would not have been humanistic because of its restricting qualities.

Prior to turning to student soliciting behavior, it should be noted that student self-relating was not discussed. Student self-relating, even more so than student self-structuring, is usually not communicated to others.

Soliciting Behavior

For students, soliciting is a major humanistic behavior because more than any other behavior it makes the student an active and involved participant in instruction. When students solicit they are sharing what is perhaps the teacher's most pervasive and controlling tool. To ask a question, to command, or to request is a venture in self-direction and responsibility, and the question is clearly a product of thought, value, or emotion. The repression of soliciting violates human capacity.

Student soliciting is of vital importance in creating and maintaining a humanistic instructional situation, but in most classrooms students are not frequent interrogators. How can student soliciting or questioning that initiates be increased? The following are suggestions for the teacher:

1. Use acquaintanceship relating behavior, select content, and provide activities that have high interest value for students. If students' curiosity is really stimulated, if their interests are really energized, students should be inclined to raise more questions.
2. Model the type of behavior the students are to display. Use the question in such a way that students come to see it as more than an oral testing procedure. Use it so that they see it as an indispensable behavior in acquiring knowledge and understanding. Make the questions honest questions—questions to which the answer is not already known. When students see the usefulness of questioning in a variety of contexts, they may employ it more frequently.
3. Be informal in classroom discourse. Teachers must not insist that students use what Barnes calls the language of the specialism or the technical language of the discipline being taught.[5] Requiring students to use the language of the specialism will inhibit their contributions. Being informal and using language which carries precise meaning for pupils should encourage student participation of all kinds, including questions. Barnes presents some evidence that it does.
4. Accept and praise student solicitations. When students do ask questions, particularly significant substantive questions, elaborate praise might encourage their continued use. Genuine praise of solicitations as well as developing, extending, or somehow using students' questions should be helpful in this direction.

Hopefully these suggestions will result in a greater quantity of student solicitations, and although all student questions can be classified as humanistic student behavior, there are some particular kinds or some specific uses of the question that increase the humanistic value of the student's question.

The reader will recall from Chapter 2 that the kinds of teacher solicitations that are humanistic are divergent, evaluative, synthesis, affectivity, convergent, analysis, and other solicitations that require and develop thinking, creating, and valuing. Some of the kinds that are nonhumanistic are cognitive-memory, translation, defining, stating, and substituting. These kinds limit and discourage thinking and valuing.

From the standpoint of the student, all of these types of solicitations, cognitive-memory as well as divergent thinking, would be humanistic, depending on how they are used. A low-level question that a student needs the answer to so that he can progress in solving a larger, more significant problem is humanistic no matter whom he asks. This type of question in this situation is appropriate for either the teacher or other students to answer. A high-level question with inquiry potential that deals with synthesis is humanistic if the student asks it of himself, if he poses it for his own inquiry. If, however, he directs it at his teacher or peers and expects a direct, straightforward response, it loses much of its humanistic character because it is requesting security and relief from freedom. Directing it at another person for purposes of clarification and gaining deeper understanding of the question or problem is a humanistic act as is using lower level, en route questions to delineate the major high-level question with inquiry potential. High-level questions with little or no inquiry potential for the teacher or another student to answer are also clearly humanistic.

Some examples of humanistic student solicitations are:

1. Student: Billy, I'm working on this problem of trading and I don't know how to spell tariff. How do you spell it?
2. Student: Why isn't everybody paid the same amount of wages, regardless of what job they have?
3. Student: Are wages and a salary the same thing, Mrs. Peterson?
4. Student: What is your reaction to the role playing incident, Janice?

These solicitations of the student are humanistic because the student is acting rather than reacting, and he is acting in ways that expand and develop his rational thought abilities. In the first and third examples he is soliciting simple facts that facilitate his inquiry into a more important matter. In the second and fourth examples the student is asking a high-level question. In the second example he is voicing a problem or concern of significance to him in an effort to get reaction and clarification from others. If he were asking it for the purpose of receiving a direct answer to the question, its humanistic qualities would be reduced. In the fourth example the student is seeking an honest answer to a high-level question with little inquiry potential.

Additional examples of humanistic student solicitations, particularly of high level solicitations with inquiry potential were presented in the previous chapter in the section on responding behavior.

Responding Behavior

Responding behavior of students is not a very important behavior in enhancing the humanistic qualities of students because of its reflexive nature. The one who is answering a question or fulfilling the expectation of a solicitation has little control over his behavior. This is especially true in the classroom where a superior-subordinate relationship exists between teacher and students. When a teacher asks a question, the student has little alternative but to attempt to answer it. Because the student has no power to control his responding behavior, and that responding is a dependent act, does not mean that responding by a student cannot be a humanistic operation. It can be humanistic depending on the type of response that is expected.

When a student is forced to engage in oral testing with the teacher in which the teacher asks specific recall or memory questions of the student, the student's human attributes are neither recognized nor developed. Not only is he placed in a dependent, irresponsible position but he is prevented from thinking for himself, from developing values, from expressing his emotions, and from creating knowledge. If, however, the teacher's question is an honest one, if it is a question to which the teacher does not already know the answer, then the student's response becomes humanistic. When the teacher solicits feeling, values, ideas, thoughts, evaluations, explanations, and inventions through initiating and developing questions, and the student's response meets the request, the response is humanistic for obvious reasons. The following are examples of these two situations. The first is nonhumanistic student responding and the second is humanistic student responding.

1. Teacher solicitation: Now, Jeff, what are the two kinds of trees we've been studying?
   Student response: The two kinds of trees are coniferous and deciduous.
2. Teacher solicitation: In your judgment are shopping centers a good thing? I mean, are we better off for having them?
   Student response: I think they are now, but we have to watch out so that we don't get too many. They take up an awful lot of land and many times they cause other shopping areas to close down.

Besides responding to the teacher, students also respond to other students. This type of responding is humanistic if the response does not limit or prevent the development of the solicitor's humanism. The criteria that apply here are the same that apply in evaluating a teacher's response as being humanistic or nonhumanistic. Direct, straightforward responses to solicitations are humanistic if the student needs the answer to the question he has asked in order to solve a larger, more important problem, the question has no inquiry potential but is an honest, sincere, high-level question, or the question calls for development of a previous response. Indirect responses are humanistic when the solicitation is a high-level question that has inquiry and developmental potential. Examples of this type of humanistic student responding are:

1. Student solicitation: Do we elect a vice-president or is he picked by the president?
   Student response: He's elected, too.
2. Student solicitation: How come it never lightnings and thunders in the winter?
   Student response: Are you positive it doesn't? Have you checked that pretty good?

Both of these responses are humanistic because, first of all, they show compassion and concern of one student for another. Further, they show the responding student to be exercising responsibility and other human qualities.

Reacting Behavior

Reacting behavior is the last student behavior to be examined in relationship to humanism. Reacting behavior refers to behavior that rates or judges or that tries to develop or extend another's comments or actions. Reacting behavior of the student in relation to a remark of the teacher or another student is a reflexive act as was student responding. The student, however, has more control over his reacting behavior than over his responding behavior. A condition for reacting behavior to occur is not a preceding solicitation or any other single behavior. A student can react to virtually any preceding behavior. In short, although there are constraints of tradition against reacting on the part of a student, the student is not kept from reacting because of the absence of some prior instructional act.

Students are free to react and ought to react much more than they do. It is a humanistic act for the student for the same reasons that informing and soliciting are. It puts the student in the position of having to exercise his independence and self-direction and to be accountable for his actions. Furthermore, it usually requires thought, value, and feeling.

The aspect of reacting that is an especially strong expression of valuing and feeling is rating. Rating means to give some form of positive or negative judgment about an idea or comment or behavior. The most humanistic rating behavior of a student is elaborate praise with explanation used to support and encourage humanistic behavior of the teacher or other students. Elaborate praise is humanistic because it communicates sincerity and caring to another person, while simple, perfunctory praise does not. Adding an explanation increases the humanism of the behavior because it appeals to reason and rational thought. Using this behavior to encourage another to use his thinking ability, to share his feelings, or to venture in a new direction is a most human act. The following are examples of this behavior:

1. Student solicitation: What did you like best about the film, Mr. Olsen?
   Teacher response: I liked the fact that there was no narration and all of us had to think for ourselves to try to discover what was happening in the film.
   Student reaction: I didn't think of that, but it's really true. That's really a neat idea. You did have to sort of guess at what's going on.
2. Student A solicitation: How come Indians live on reservations? Why don't they just live in cities with everyone else?
   Student B reaction: That's an interesting question, Peggy! I'd really like to investigate that one myself. It will be a good project.

Each of these reactions carries elaborate praise and explanations.

The other aspect of reacting is developing. Developing another's ideas or thoughts by probing, clarifying, extending and through other actions is a humanistic behavior of students as well as teachers. Developing reacting is a humanistic act because in addition to its being a self-directed act on the part of the person who is using the behavior, it facilitates rational thought and value clarification of the person who receives it. Although some forms of developing reacting such as controlling thought and nonauthentic data extenders, as mentioned in Chapter 2, are nonhumanistic, developing reacting is basically a humanistic behavior for the student. Some examples of it are:

1. Student solicitation: Do you think the world would be different if cars had never been invented?
   Teacher response: No, I think things would be fairly much the same.
   Student reaction: Well, why? How could they be the same?
2. Student A solicitation: What character in the story would you most like to be, Kathy?
   Student B response: I'd like to be the older daughter or maybe the father.
   Student A reaction: Why do these two roles appeal to you?

These are examples of lifting thought. In each case the student's reaction calls for explanation and justification of the preceding behavior.

If students engage in reacting behavior such as this as well as in informing and soliciting behavior, the partial role reversal of teachers and students will be complete and humanistic instruction will become more of a reality. Thus far, humanistic teacher behavior and humanistic student behavior have been treated more or less separately. The purpose of the next chapter is to rejoin these two sets of behavior in the form of a review and examine a more lengthy segment of instruction to further illustrate humanistic behavior in the classroom.

Notes

1. Fyodor Dostoevsky, "Notes from the Underground," *The Short Novels of Dostoevsky*. Translated by Constance Garnett. (New York: Dial Press, 1945), p. 46.
2. Henry David Thoreau, *Walden* (New York: New American Library, Inc., 1942), p. 216.
3. Louis E. Raths, Merrill Harmon, and Sidney B. Simon, *Values and Teaching: Working with Values in the Classroom* (Columbus, Ohio: Charles E. Merrill Books, Inc., 1966).
4. Arno A. Bellack, *et. al.*, *The Language of the Classroom* (New York: Teachers College Press, 1966).
5. Douglas Barnes, *Language, the Learner and the School* (Baltimore: Penguin Books, Inc., 1969).

The Humanistic Encounter: A Review

A humanistic encounter between teacher and students is relatively easy to talk about in general and often stereotyped terms. It is more difficult, but infinitely more useful, to describe specific humanistic classroom behaviors of teachers and students. To identify and describe in detail behaviors of classroom participants that are humanistic in an effort to influence teachers to make their teaching-learning situations humanistic encounters is the major goal of this book.

Both humanistic teacher behavior and humanistic student behavior have been examined in detail in previous chapters. The purpose of this chapter is to synthesize the significant aspects of humanistic behavior in the classroom.

Summarizing Humanistic Behavior

For the interactive situation to be a humanistic one, teachers and students need to behave in the following ways in relation to the acts of informing, soliciting, responding, and reacting:

1. Informing: structuring

    To make classroom encounters more humanistic, structuring needs to be:

    a. Used more frequently by students and less frequently by teachers than it normally is used.

    b. Open and general rather than closed and specific, when done for others. Employing fewer and broader elements is generally more humanistic. However, structuring that includes many specific elements can be humanistic if it is used for a short duration and results in a larger humanistic end, or if it is self-structuring or cooperative structuring.

2. Informing: relating

To make classroom encounters more humanistic, relating needs to be:

a. Used more frequently by students and less frequently by teachers than it normally is used.
b. Familiarizing or facilitating rather than inculcating or internalizing for others. Familiarizing should be interpreted somewhat more broadly for students than for teachers. When students engage in familiarizing, it may be less deliberate than teacher familiarizing. It may take the form of supporting propositions, introducing new points, or recounting past experiences without being requested to do so.

3. Soliciting

To make classroom encounters more humanistic, soliciting needs to be:

a. Used more frequently by students and less frequently by teachers than it normally is used.
b. High level with many appropriate response possibilities for the purpose of clarification if the question has inquiry potential or for a sincere "honest" response if it does not. High level, many response possibility solicitations with inquiry potential are not humanistic if they are employed to receive a direct answer from the teacher or a student.
c. Low level with one or few response possibilities for the purpose of obtaining factual information which will clarify or facilitate the solution of a more significant inquiry problem.

4. Responding

To make classroom encounters more humanistic, responding needs to be:

a. Used less frequently by students in response to the teacher and more frequently by teachers than it normally is used.
b. Direct to factual, en route questions that facilitate solution of a major problem, to high-level initiating questions that have no inquiry potential, and to developmental questions that extend, lift, or clarify previous responses of the teacher or other students. Direct responses to inquiry potential solicitations or to questions that seek to place the respondent in an oral testing situation are not humanistic.
c. Indirect to inquiry solicitations and to oral testing type solicitations. Indirect responses to factual, en route questions, to

developmental questions, or to noninquiry potential high-level questions of student or teacher are not humanistic.

5. Reacting: rating

   To make classroom encounters more humanistic, rating needs to be:
   a. Used more frequently by students and less frequently by teachers than it normally is used.
   b. Elaborate praise with explanations. Perfunctory praise by student or teacher is not humanistic.

6. Reacting: developing

   To make classroom encounters more humanistic, developing needs to be:
   a. Used more frequently by students and by teachers than it normally is used.
   b. Lifting, extending, and clarifying. Developing that controls is not humanistic.

To prescribe specific humanistic behavior of teachers and of students is important and useful in creating humanistic encounters, but the problem of how to bring about these behaviors in classrooms remains. Fortunately, a circular relationship exists between the teacher and students in the classroom. Hughes speaks of this relationship as mutual influence.[1] Teachers influence students and students influence teachers. Teacher power is a measure of teacher influence while teacher responsiveness is a measure of student influence. Classroom participants do not have equal influence, however. Teachers have the major responsibility for the education of students and, therefore, have greater influence than students. Because of the teacher's position of authority he can initiate humanistic instruction. It is reasonable to assume that his use of humanistic behavior will result in greater use of humanistic behaviors by students which will, in turn, encourage greater use of humanistic behaviors by the teacher. If the teacher's goal is humanistic teaching, the student's goal will soon become humanistic "studenting." Each participant's behavior will serve as feedback input to the other until a humanistic classroom situation exists.

More specifically, this circular relationship serves to develop and sustain humanistic instruction in the following ways. When teachers use open, general structuring, student structuring for others and student self-structuring are encouraged as is relating and soliciting of students. The use of familiarizing and facilitating relating at appropriate times by teachers increases the occurrence of student soliciting, developing reacting, and student relating. Reduced soliciting by teachers and soliciting designed to clarify and facilitate student inquiry results in increased student soliciting, relating, and humanistic types of responding. When teachers use elaborate praise following student behavior that is humanistic the likelihood of its recurrence is increased. Finally, the use of lifting and extending reacting behavior by teachers encourages appropriate responding, developing, soliciting, and other behaviors performed in a humanistic way by students. As the students begin to react to humanistic behavior of the teacher by structuring class situations; by initiating ideas, experiences, and views; by posing many high-level and also low-level questions at appropriate times; by responding only to solicitations that meet the criteria of humanistic instruction; by rating the teacher's ideas as well as other students; and by lifting and extending others' thoughts or viewpoints, the teacher's humanistic behavior is reinforced and he is stimulated to increase his humanistic behavior. The more students ask questions, the more responding and the less questioning by the teacher. The more students relate or develop others' responses, the less relating and developing he does. The more structuring and rating that students provide, the less he provides. In a sense, what happens as the teacher and students begin to move toward humanistic instruction is that teachers and students both become learners and teachers. The relationship becomes more of an equal one in which all classroom participants share responsibility for each other's growth.

The Humanistic Encounter: Transcript and Analysis

Although numerous examples have been given of the various teacher and student humanistic behaviors, most of these examples were brief and isolated. To provide a clearer understanding of humanistic instruction, a complete transcribed session of a Gestalt game lesson, Landlord and Tenant, is included here. The reader is referred to Chapter 5 for a description of this particular game. As will be seen in the analysis and discussion of the lesson which follows the transcript, this teacher is moving toward humanistic instruction but has some improvement to make in creating a wholly humanistic interactive situation.

LANDLORD AND TENANT

Teacher: (1) This morning, boys and girls, we're going to act out a meeting between a landlord and a tenant. The tenant is going to be evicted by the landlord. Jim and Will volunteered to be the two actors yesterday and have made mental lists of some of the things they might say to each other. Now here's the scene: the landlord is just about to knock on the door of the tenant's apartment. When the tenant opens the door, the landlord goes in and tells the tenant to move. The tenant asks why and then the confrontation begins. Now, should we begin with the knock, boys.

Will: (knock-knock) Mr. Jones, are you in?

Jim: Oh, Mr. Narth, what do you want?

Will: I'm sorry, but I'm going to have to ask you to move out of this apartment by Saturday.

Jim: Move out! What are you talking about? I can't move out. What right have you got to ask me to move out?

Will: It's your complaining all the time. You're always shooting off your mouth. I've decided that since you don't like it here, it's time for you to get your stuff together and get out! I've fixed the roof for you and all you do is complain.

Jim: Sure, you've had it fixed, but it still leaks. Look at that wall there. You got such a two-bit man to do the work. He did a sloppy job. Look at my dresser there I just bought. It's messed up because of the water on the varnish.

Will: I can't help that. I paid the roofer good enough money, but he just didn't do a good job.

Jim: You should have enough money to hire a better roofer, all the money we pay you.

Will: Well, $75.00 is not much money. I plan to raise the rent for the new people who are coming. The rent I get from this apartment isn't enough to do all the repairs. The basement needs fixing too.

Jim: Well, you shouldn't have bought the building then.

Will: I need money, too. I like making money, too.

Jim: Well, you should fix the place if you want to make money.

Will: That's my business. Besides, complaining isn't all. The neighbors have been talking about the drinking and parties you've been having. With all the noise, they can't sleep.

Jim: I pay good money to live here, I can do anything I wish. Who's doing the talking anyway?

Will: It doesn't matter. The point is you're disturbing other people.

Jim: Well, O.K. I'm sorry if I'm disturbing other people, but I still don't think I'm any noisier than all those little brats around here. Why don't you talk to the parents of all those kids? They wreck a lot of stuff, too.

Will: I'm not here to talk about other people, I'm here to tell you to get out by Saturday. And, one more thing, talking about wrecking things, you're dog has made a mess out of the lawn. You know I only permit small house dogs, and they are never to be chained up outside.

Jim: I never chain him up. Sometimes he just runs away from me when I take him out for a walk. I can't help it if he digs up your stupid grass. Are you an animal hater? I know you hate people.

Will: That's enough. You be out by Saturday and that's final!

Jim: But.

Will: No buts, OUT!

Teacher: (2) That was excellent role playing, boys. You really did a good job. You've brought up some very interesting aspects of the relationship of a landlord to a tenant.

(3) Let's get into this issue further now.

(4) How do you feel about this argument we've just seen?

Terri: (5) I agree with the landlord. I think the tenant should be evicted.

Teacher: (6) Why do you support the landlord, Terri?

Terri: (7) Well, it does cost a lot of money to repair a building and keep it in good shape. If the landlord hadn't tried to fix the roof, that would be a different story. But, he *did* hire somebody to do it. He can't help it if the roofer was a crummy worker.

(8) You get a lot of men who don't do good jobs. We just had our portable T.V. in the T.V. shop for two weeks, and when we got it back it still didn't work right. And, it wasn't a cheap place either.

Carol: (9) But just because the tenant complained a little, is that a good reason to kick him out?

Terri: (10) I think it is. It sounds like this guy complains a lot— like he'd complain no matter what. Even if the roof had been fixed right, he'd still complain probably.

Carol: (11) I still don't see why!

Terri: (12) The landlord is just going to have trouble with this guy all the time, and so will the other renters. He should be kicked out now before his complaining and crabbiness drives other renters away.

Walt: (13) Yah, Terri, but how would you feel if somebody kicked you out of your home?

Terri: (14) I wouldn't like it. That's why I wouldn't be a complaining renter.

Teacher: (15) Other reactions to the incident?

HUMANISTIC ENCOUNTER: A REVIEW 69

Joseph: (16) I think the landlord is right, too. It sounds as though the tenant doesn't follow the rules of the building besides all of his complaining.
Teacher: (17) Go on. Tell us more, Joseph.
Joseph: (18) Well, I mean he has parties where there is loud drinking and his dog makes a mess on the grass. This is breaking the rules of the building. He knew what the rules were before he moved in. If he thought they were bad rules he could have tried to change them at that time. Now he's got to follow them or leave.
Scott: (19) That's a good point, Joe. I agree with you.
(20) If the landlord lets one person get away with breaking the rules, others will want to break them, too. Then it really starts. Everybody does whatever they please and pretty soon the whole place falls down.
Teacher: (21) Are there any other arguments in support of the landlord? Alicia?
Alicia: (22) Well, I'm for the landlord, but not because of the reasons given. Those reasons are not bad enough to make the guy move. If the renter didn't pay the rent or was really a hood or something I'd kick him out. The way this guy sounded he could have been a drug pusher or gambler.
Teacher: (23) If you evict him because you think he's a hood, but you have no verifiable evidence, you're denying his rights, aren't you? It's for the courts to decide if he's guilty, isn't it?
Alicia: (24) Yes, but if I saw him smoking pot or something I'd call the police and get him out of the building at the same time. Who would rent my apartments if they saw one of my tenants smoking pot? No one, that's who! I'd have to protect myself and the other tenants.
Teacher: (25) Have you thought carefully about the idea of punishing someone without a hearing or trial?
Alicia: (26) Well, yes. I guess so.
Tom: (27) Mr. Thompson, I think Alicia said a good thing about the rent.
(28) If the rent isn't paid the landlord has no choice but to make the tenant leave.
Sue: (29) But what if the tenant had been out of work because of sickness and didn't have the money? Wouldn't you be willing to wait for your money then?
Tom: (30) But the landlord has bills too.
(31) Do you think the people the landlord owes money to would be willing to wait for their money?
Sue: (32) I think they would if he explained to them.

Hanover: (33) Except for Sue's comments, we've heard several arguments that favor the landlord; what about the tenant? Who favors the tenant? What arguments favor the tenant?

Carol: (34) Well, I think the tenant should be allowed to stay. He had a perfect right to complain about the roof. His dresser and probably other things were damaged by the leaking water. He *should* complain about that. Maybe if the roof isn't fixed right it'll get worse and cost more money. The landlord should want to know about the leaking.

Sara: (35) Maybe the apartment building has other problems, too. It might have rats or cockroaches.

(36) Don't you think the landlord would want to know about the rats or cockroaches, Mr. Thompson?

Teacher: (37) Yes. I do.

Sara: (38) Ugh. They look so horrible. The landlord would hate to have them.

Teacher: (39) Why? How does looking horrible cause harm? What is harmful about rats and cockroaches, about their looking horrible or about any other aspect of them?

Sara: (40) Um, I guess I don't know. I have some hunches but I'd like to look into this further.

(41) Is Will Kill Exterminators in the yellow pages, do you think?

Loree: (42) Yes. I'm sure it is, Sara.

Robby: (43) I think the tenant's strongest case is the short notice. Asking somebody to leave by Saturday is probably less than a week away and that's unfair.

Teacher: (44) Why?

Robby: (45) Well, he couldn't get another place to live by Saturday, and I know that it sometimes takes months to get a mover to come.

Mark: (46) And another thing is that it's against the law. You have to give a tenant a certain amount of time before you have him get out. I think it's one month.

Teacher: (47) What if he had a lease for one year and it was up on Saturday? Would the landlord then be justified in his action?

Robby: (48) I still think he should give him a longer notice than a week. It's only fair.

Karl: (49) Mr. Thompson, I've heard about the law that Mark mentioned. I wonder, do most landlords follow it? Are they honest?

HUMANISTIC ENCOUNTER: A REVIEW 71

Teacher: (50) That's an excellent question that could be pursued in greater depth, Karl.
(51) I wonder if there is such a law. If so, I wonder who it applies to and what type of law it is.
Karl: (52) I'm going to ask our landord, Mr. Howell, about it tonight and then tomorrow noon I'm going to check two other apartment buildings next to ours.
Teacher: (53) Great, Karl. It's really an interesting problem. Talking to your landlord is a good idea.
(54) Maybe some of the others would like to work on that with you. I'll help in any way I can.
Betsy: (55) Mr. Thompson, what do you think about the tenant?
Teacher: (56) My personal feeling is that he should be permitted to stay.
Betsy: (57) Well, what are your reasons?
Teacher: (58) From the role playing it's my guess that this may be the first confrontation between the landlord and the tenant, and I believe everyone should have a second chance.
Betsy: (59) That's a good idea. I never thought of that.
Teacher: (60) I'm glad you like it, Betsy.
(61) Darlene, what are your thoughts?
Darlene: (62) Well, concerning Hanover's question, this is like your reason, but the man did say he was sorry for the loud party. Maybe if the landlord had asked him to pay for the damages to the lawn and had promised to fix the roof they both would have been calmer and they wouldn't have gotten so mad.
Teacher: (63) Go on, what is your reason then, Darlene?
Darlene: (64) Well, the tenant is the guy who really loses in this situation, and what I'm saying is he did say he was sorry and probably would have paid for the damages and promised to behave himself if the landlord had asked him rather than just storming in there and kicking him out.
P. J.: (65) I agree with Darlene all the way. The landlord had too much of a chip on his shoulder.
Terri: (66) What do you mean? It was the tenant who had a chip on his shoulder. He had a whole log on it, if you ask me.
Teacher: (67) What's happening here? What's beginning to come out of our discussion?
Carol: (68) Well, they are both right and they're both wrong. Each man is at fault in some ways for what has happened.
Bob: (69) There are two sides to every story.

Teacher: (70) Could you explain that further, Bob?
Bob: (71) Um, when you look at the situation or what caused this incident you can look at it from the landlord's side and from the tenant's side. And, whatever side you're looking from seems like the right one at the time.
Linda: (72) Mr. Thompson, I think I know how this situation might be solved without making the tenant leave.
Teacher: (73) Let's hear your solution, Linda.
Linda: (74) Well, it's really what Darlene was sort of saying. Each of the men could agree to give a little. The landlord could agree to fix the roof better and get the dresser fixed and the tenant could pay for damages to the grass and promise to change and be a nicer person. They could bargain with each other.
Terri: (75) Why would the landlord go along with that?
Linda: (76) Well this way he wouldn't lose any rent waiting for a new tenant and also he wouldn't have to spend money to redecorate for new people.
Teacher: (77) Bargaining is a very good idea.
(78) Scott?
Scott: (79) My idea is that maybe if the tenant has lots of friends in the apartment building he could get together with them and they could form a group. If one gets kicked out for no good reason, they'll all leave.
Steve: (80) Or the tenant and the landlord could each get lawyers, and the lawyers could settle it in court the right way.
Chris: (81) I think the situation may be impossible to settle now, or maybe they could still do this. Each needs to make a list of his rules or things that are important and the other agree to them. Only when this happens will the landlord let the tenant move in and will the tenant want to move in. I guess what I'm saying is that there should be a contract or I think they call it a lease.
Teacher: (82) Those are all good thoughts. It's not an easy situation to solve, that's sure.
P. J.: (83) What time is art today, Mr. Thompson?
Teacher: (84) Mrs. Peters will be coming at 11:00.
P. J.: (85) Then I suppose we'd better stop and get ready because it's eleven now. I'd like to continue tomorrow, though, but I can't speak for the others.

To facilitate the analysis of this lesson the prescriptions for humanistic classroom behavior of teachers and students have been developed into an analysis instrument presented in Table I. Other types of instruments may have emerged from the same prescriptions and after extended use this one may need alteration, but it serves the purpose of analyzing this particular lesson and further explaining the nature of humanistic instruction. As can be seen in Table I the instrument contains twelve major categories: six for the teachers and six for the students. Each of these is further divided into two subcategories. The first subcategory for each category represents humanistic behavior, while the second represents nonhumanistic behavior.

The procedure in using the instrument is to identify behaviors and then assign a number to the behavior that represents the category to which the behavior belongs. A behavior, the unit of analysis, can be as short as one word or as long a several paragraphs. Each utterance of a teacher or of a student is one behavior for as long as the teacher or student continues to perform the same act such as structuring or responding. Each change or shift in the interaction from structuring to soliciting or from soliciting to responding, for example, represents a new behavior. Each of the behaviors that occurred in the preceding transcript, with the exception of the role-playing incident, has been identified and numbered chronologically. In Table II these behaviors are described and classified. Table III summarizes the results of the analysis.

It can be seen from these two tables of results that a partial role reversal did take place in the lesson. Students did engage in many of the behaviors that are usually performed by the teacher and the teacher displayed some behaviors that are usually only used by students. Although the teacher structured in this lesson he only did it four times while students structured twice. No relating was done at all by the teacher but students did considerable relating. They volunteered substantive information eleven times. In relation to soliciting, the teacher asked only five questions. This is actually fewer than the eight questions asked by the students.

The responding behavior of students was extensive. They responded more than anything else. These twenty-four behaviors are not as much cause for concern as they seem to be on the surface. From Table IV it can be seen that nine of these responses were to questions of other students and that nine of the responses to teacher's questions were to developmental questions. Only six responses were to teacher initiating solicitations. This means that of the twenty-four student responses, a good portion are the result of humanistic acts on the part of the teacher and other students. The teacher's five responses contrast sharply with the students' twenty-four, but actually five is quite prominent. He used responding as much if not more than any other behavior with the exception of developing.

Table I
AN INSTRUMENT FOR ASSESSING HUMANISTIC INSTRUCTIONAL BEHAVIOR

Teacher Behavior
1.0 Informing: structuring
   1.1 Open, general
   1.2 Closed, specific
2.0 Informing: relating
   2.1 Familiarizing—facilitating
   2.2 Inculcating—internalizing
3.0 Soliciting
   3.1 High level, usually many responses
   3.2 Low level, usually one response
4.0 Responding
   4.1 Direct to en route questions, developmental questions, and high-level initiating questions unless high-level question has inquiry potential. Indirect to inquiry questions.
   4.2 Indirect to en route questions, developmental questions, and high-level initiating questions unless high-level question has inquiry potential. Direct to inquiry questions.
5.0 Reacting: rating
   5.1 Elaborate with explanation for humanistic behavior
   5.2 Perfunctory
6.0 Reacting: developing
   6.1 Lifting-extending-clarifying
   6.2 Controlling

Student Behavior
1.0 Informing: structuring
   1.1 Open, general for others
       Closed, specific for self or cooperatively with others
   1.2 Open, general for self
       Closed, specific for others
2.0 Informing: relating
   2.1 Familiarizing—facilitating
   2.2 Inculcating—internalizing
3.0 Soliciting
   3.1 High level, usually many responses for clarification or for honest answer
       Low level, usually one response for facilitating or clarification of inquiry problem
   3.2 High level, usually many responses with inquiry potential for direct answer
4.0 Responding
   4.1 Direct to en route questions, developmental questions, and high-level initiating questions unless high-level question has inquiry potential
       Indirect to inquiry questions and oral testing questions

       4.2 Indirect to en route questions, developmental questions, and high-level initiating questions unless high-level question has inquiry potential
           Direct to inquiry questions and oral testing questions
5.0 Reacting: rating
       5.1 Elaborate with explanation for humanistic behavior
       5.2 Perfunctory
6.0 Reacting: developing
       6.1 Lifting–extending–clarifying
       6.2 Controlling

TABLE II

TRANSCRIPT ANALYSIS: LANDLORD AND TENANT

Behavior	Description	Classification
1	Teacher uses structuring behavior that consists of many, fairly specific elements	T1.2–Informing: structuring– Closed, specific
2	Teacher praises role playing and gives reasons for praise	T5.1–Reacting: rating– Elaborate with explanation
3	Teacher uses structuring behavior that consists of few, general elements	T1.1–Informing: structuring– Open, general
4	Teacher asks broad open question that calls for evaluation	T3.1–Soliciting–High level
5	Student responds with evaluative answer	S4.1–Responding–Direct to high-level question
6	Teacher calls for support for student's response	T6.1–Reacting: developing –Lifting
7	Student responds with support to teacher's developing	S4.1–Responding–Direct to developmental question
8	Student initiates analogy	S2.1–Informing: relating– Familiarizing
9	Student calls for justification of other student's response	S6.1–Reacting: developing –Lifting
10	Student responds with justification to other student's developing	S4.1–Responding–Direct to developmental question
11	Student calls for additional justification of other student's response	S6.1–Reacting: developing –Lifting

12	Student responds with justification or explanation to other student's developing	S4.1—Responding—Direct to developmental question
13	Student asks affective question of another student	S3.1—Soliciting—High level
14	Student responds with affective answer	S4.1—Responding—Direct to high-level question
15	Teacher restates initial, initiating solicitation (Behavior No. 4)	T3.1—Soliciting—High level
16	Student responds with evaluative answer	S4.1—Responding—Direct to high-level question
17	Teacher calls for extension of student's response	T6.1—Reacting: developing —Extending
18	Student responds with an extension of his first response	S4.1—Responding—Direct to developmental question
19	Student praises another student's response but gives no reason	S5.1—Reacting: rating— Elaborate praise
20	Student initiates statement that extends previous response (Behavior No. 18)	S2.1—Informing: relating— Familiarizing
21	Teacher restates initial, initiating solicitation (Behavior No. 4) in somewhat narrower terms but solicitation is still evaluative	T3.1—Soliciting—High level
22	Student responds with evaluative answer and support for it	S4.1—Responding—Direct to high-level question
23	Teacher calls for value clarification	T6.1—Reacting: developing —Clarifying
24	Student persists in his views rather than reflect on teacher's clarification question	S4.2—Responding—Indirect to developmental question
25	Teacher calls for value clarification again	T6.1—Reacting: developing —Clarifying
26	Student responds with reflective statement	S4.1—Responding—Direct to developmental question
27	Student praises another student's response but gives no reasons	S5.1—Reacting: rating— Elaborate praise

28	Student initiates statement of conclusion	S2.1—Informing: relating—Familiarizing
29	Student calls for re-thinking of other student's response through a challenging question	S6.1—Reacting: developing—Extending
30	Student responds by challenging rather than with an honest answer	S4.2—Responding—Indirect to developmental question
31	Student initiates analysis or evaluative question directed at another student	S3.1—Soliciting—High level
32	Student responds with analysis	S4.1—Responding—Direct to high-level question
33	Student asks a broad, open question calling for evaluation which changes the topic of discussion	S3.1—Soliciting—High level
34	Student responds with evaluation	S4.1—Responding—Direct to high-level question
35	Student initiates statement that extends previous response (Behavior No. 34)	S2.1—Informing: relating—Familiarizing
36	Student asks an opinion or convergent question of the teacher	S3.1—Soliciting—High level
37	Teacher responds with an opinion	T4.1—Responding—Direct to high-level question
38	Student contributes additional viewpoints that extend previous comments (Behavior No. 35)	S2.1—Informing: relating—Familiarizing
39	Teacher attempts to develop student's thinking and identify an inquiry problem	T6.1—Reacting: developing—Lifting
40	Student responds by expressing interest in the problem	S4.1—Responding—Direct to developmental questions
41	Student asks recall question that will facilitate solution of the problem	S3.1—Soliciting—Low level
42	Student responds by providing requested information	S4.1—Responding—Direct to en route question

43	Student responds with evaluative answer to previous solicitation (Behavior No. 33)	S4.1—Responding—Direct to high-level question
44	Teacher calls for justification of student's response	T6.1—Reacting: developing —Lifting
45	Student responds with justification	S4.1—Responding—Direct to developmental question
46	Student introduces idea that extends previous response (Behavior No. 45)	S2.1—Informing: relating— Familiarizing
47	Teacher attempts to clarify student's idea by challenging it	T6.1—Reacting: developing —Extending
48	Student responds with opinion	S4.1—Responding—Direct to developmental question
49	Student poses evaluative question with research potential	S3.1—Soliciting—High level
50	Teacher praises student's question that has inquiry potential	T5.1—Reacting: rating— Elaborate praise with explanation
51	Teacher responds with statements to help student clarify problem	T4.1—Responding—Indirect to inquiry potential question
52	Student structures his future behavior in an attempt to gather data for his problem	S1.1—Informing: structuring —Closed, specific for self
53	Teacher praises student's problem and procedures	T5.1—Reacting: rating— Elaborate praise with explanation
54	Teacher structures future behavior of other students and himself in open, general way	T1.1—Informing: structuring —Open, general
55	Student asks evaluative question of the teacher	S3.1—Solicitating—High level
56	Teacher responds with personal viewpoint	T4.1—Responding—Direct to high-level question
57	Student requests teacher to support his viewpoint	S6.1—Reacting: developing —Lifting

58	Teacher responds with support	T4.1—Responding—Direct to developmental question
59	Student praises teacher's response	S5.1—Reacting: rating—Elaborate praise with explanation
60	Teacher praises student's role reversal behavior	T5.1—Reacting: rating—Elaborate praise
61	Teacher restates previous question through implication (Behavior No. 33)	T3.1—Soliciting—High level
62	Student responds by giving judgment	S4.1—Responding—Direct to high-level question
63	Teacher requests student to respond further	T6.1—Reacting: developing—Extending
64	Student responds with extension	S4.1—Responding—Direct to developmental question
65	Student praises other student's response in a nonperfunctory way	S5.1—Reacting: rating—Elaborate praise with explanation
66	Student calls for justification of previous student's remarks	S6.1—Reacting: developing—Extending
67	Teacher poses convergent thinking, conclusion drawing question	T3.1—Solicitating—High level
68	Student responds by giving conclusion	S4.1—Responding—Direct to high-level question
69	Student responds by giving conclusion	S4.1—Responding—Direct to high-level question
70	Teacher calls for additional comments from student	T6.1—Reacting: developing—Extending
71	Student responds with extension of his point	S4.1—Responding—Direct to developmental question
72	Student initiates new idea or solution	S2.1—Informing: relating—Familiarizing
73	Teacher calls for description of student's solution	T6.1—Reacting: developing—Extending

74	Student continues to relate her solution	S2.1—Informing: relating—Familiarizing
75	Student calls for explanation of other student's idea	S6.1—Reacting: developing—Lifting
76	Student responds with explanation	S4.1—Responding—Direct to developmental question
77	Teacher praises student's idea	T5.1—Reacting: rating—Elaborate praise
78	Teacher recognizes student's desire to make a statement	T1.1—Informing: structuring—Open, general
79	Student volunteers solution	S2.1—Informing: relating—Familiarizing
80	Student volunteers solution	S2.1—Informing: relating—Familiarizing
81	Student volunteers solution	S2.1—Informing: relating—Familiarizing
82	Teacher praises all three solutions	T5.1—Reacting: rating—Elaborate praise with explanation
83	Student asks procedural question of teacher	S3.1—Soliciting—Low level for facilitation
84	Teacher meets student's request	T4.1—Responding—Direct to type of en route question
85	Student brings closure to the session and looks ahead to the future	S1.1—Informing: structuring: Open, general

TABLE III
A SUMMARY OF THE TRANSCRIPT ANALYSIS

Teacher Behavior			Student Behavior		
Categories	Frequency	Behavior	Categories	Frequency	Behavior
1.0	4	1, 3, 54, 78	1.0	2	52, 85
1.1	3	3, 54, 78	1.1	2	52, 85
1.2	1	1	1.2	0	
2.0	0		2.0	11	8, 20, 28, 35, 38, 46, 72, 74, 79, 80, 81
2.1	0		2.1	11	8, 20, 28, 35, 38, 46, 72, 74, 79, 80, 81
2.2	0		2.2	0	
3.0	5	4, 15, 21, 61, 67	3.0	8	13, 31, 33, 36, 41, 49, 55, 83
3.1	5	4, 15, 21, 61, 67	3.1	8	13, 31, 33, 36, 41, 49, 55, 83
3.2	0		3.2	0	
4.0	5	37, 51, 56, 58, 84	4.0	24	5, 7, 10, 12, 14, 16, 18, 22, 24, 26, 30, 32, 34, 40, 42, 43, 45, 48, 62, 64, 68, 69, 71, 76
4.1	5	37, 51, 56, 58, 84	4.1	22	5, 7, 10, 12, 14, 16, 18, 22, 26, 32, 34, 40, 42, 43, 45, 48, 62, 64, 68, 69, 71, 76
4.2	0		4.2	2	24, 30
5.0	6	2, 50, 53, 60, 77, 82	5.0	4	19, 27, 59, 65
5.1	6	2, 50, 53, 60, 77, 82	5.1	4	19, 27, 59, 65
5.2	0		5.2	0	
6.0	10	6, 17, 23, 25, 39, 44, 47, 63, 70, 73	6.0	6	9, 11, 29, 57, 66, 75
6.1	10	6, 17, 23, 25, 39, 44, 47, 63, 70, 73	6.1	6	9, 11, 29, 57, 66, 75
6.2	0		6.2	0	
Total Behaviors	30		Total Behaviors	55	

TABLE IV
STUDENT RESPONSES

Type of Responding	Frequency	Behavior
To teacher's initiating solicitation	6	5, 16, 22, 62, 68, 69
To teacher's developing reaction	9	7, 18, 24, 26, 40, 45, 48, 64, 71
To student's initiating solicitation	4	14, 32, 34, 43
To student's developing reaction	5	10, 12, 30, 42, 76
Total student responses	24	

Rating behavior of the teacher and of students was similar in quantity. Students rated others four times and teachers issued ratings six times. These totals are consistent with the concept of role reversal as are the totals for developing. The teacher developed students' responses ten times while students developed the teacher's or other students' responses six times.

A closer examination of Tables II and III reveals that not only did the teacher and students exchange roles to a great degree, but most of the specific behaviors displayed in the lesson were humanistic behaviors. Of the structuring behavior, all that occurred was humanistic with one exception. That exception was the teacher's first structuring behavior. It is not humanistic per se because, although it serves a necessary purpose in launching the role-playing experience, it contains many specific elements. By itself, however, it does not appreciably alter the humanistic encounter. Had a pattern of structuring like this emerged in the lesson, humanism would have been seriously reduced. All of the other teacher structuring behavior was open. It contained very few elements and the elements that were used were general. The two times a student structured, the structuring contained several specific elements, but the structuring was for the student who was doing it and, therefore, is consistent with humanism. The second of the two behaviors also contains some structuring for the class. This structuring contains some specific elements, but it still is more open than closed.

With no exception all of the relating behavior was humanistic. At no time was it employed simply to have others take in and remember information. Of the eleven times that students used it, it was used to familiarize other students and the teacher with an idea or point of view. Relating for the purpose of facilitating the solution of a problem was not employed.

The soliciting behavior of the teacher and the students was totally humanistic. Each of the teacher's five questions was a high-level question requiring productive thought of students. Four of these requested evaluation and one convergent thought. They all permitted great freedom in responding. Of the students' eight solicitations, four were directed at other students and four at the teacher. Those directed at other students called for evaluation, affective response, or remembered information to facilitate the solution of a problem. The questions the students asked of the teacher requested opinion, evaluation, and procedural information. One of these had inquiry potential and it was asked for purposes of clarification.

The responding behavior of the teacher and the students was almost totally humanistic. All of the teacher's responding behavior was humanistic, but two responses of the students were not. The teacher's five responses consisted of giving direct responses to two high-level initiating questions and to a development question and an en route question. The teacher gave an indirect response only once, and that was to a question that had potential for inquiry. The teacher did not respond indirectly to developing or facilitating questions nor did he attempt to provide straightforward answers to questions that students could profitably develop into research projects. The majority of the students' responses were direct answers to either high-level initiating questions or to developmental questions of the teacher or other students. The two instances of nonhumanistic responding were both indirect answers to developmental questions. In both cases an attempt was made to clarify or extend a previous response, but the responding student persisted in his original position without considering the requested development.

Of the rating behavior that was displayed in the lesson, all of it was elaborate but not all of it contained reasons or explorations concerning why the preceding behavior was praiseworthy. It is particularly interesting to note that not one perfunctory rating was issued during this lesson by either the teacher or students. The reader will recall from Chapter 2 that in most lessons teachers use perfunctory rating very frequently.

The developing behavior of the teacher and students also meets the criteria for humanistic classroom behavior with no exception. The teacher attempted to extend or clarify thought seven times and lift it three times. He did not try to control students' thoughts at any time. The students' developing was mostly directed at other students and attempted to both lift and extend. In one instance a student lifted the teacher's previous response.

The teacher and students involved in this lesson concerning confrontation between a landlord and a tenant have employed behaviors and created a situation that is very close to a totally humanistic encounter. To more fully achieve the goal of humanistic instruction the students' responding behavior should be reduced even further, that is responding to teacher initiating solicitations, and his soliciting and developing be increased. Further, the teacher, through extending and lifting developing and possibly elaborate rating, should try to extract and develop more problems that interest and stimulate students to the point where they will want to begin an investigation immediately. Also, greater use of the teacher by the students to obtain information or clarify ideas through both high-level and low-level solicitations and through development reacting as well as greater use of students by students for these same and other purposes would increase the humanism of the encounter.

Although the interactive behavior of the teacher and the students is a most significant element in the humanistic teaching and learning situation, if not the most significant, humanistic teacher behavior and humanistic student behavior do not equal a totally humanistic situation. The milieu in which the interaction occurs must also be considered. A very important aspect of that milieu is the substance or content of the message that is communicated This content as well as the method with which it is sent and received can be either humanistic or nonhumanistic. The next section deals with the content of humanistic instruction and strategies for implementing humanistic instruction.

Notes

1. Marie M. Hughes and Associates. *The Assessment of the Quality of Teaching: A Research Report.* U. S. Office of Education, Cooperative Research Project No. 353. (Salt Lake City: University of Utah, 1959).

Part III

Making Humanistic Instruction a Reality: Content and Strategies

In Part I of this book, we discussed general goals by identifying the characteristics of humanism. In Part II, humanistic instructional behavior on the part of teachers and students was described in a more specific manner. A major objective for this section was to provide the reader with more specific examples of humanistic behavior in order to define humanistic education more concretely. In Part III, we intend to focus on humanistic content or subject matter and describe strategies or approaches that we feel are most promising in order to encourage humanism in elementary school classrooms. The term *strategies* simply refers to overall plans an individual or group employs in order to achieve desired goals.

All strategies have four components in common: *objectives,* either expressed or tacit; *methods or procedures* adopted in order to achieve objectives; *materials;* and *evaluation measures* which are used in order to see how close one is to the goals. We will discuss what we have judged to be two of the most promising strategies or approaches for implementing both humanistic content and humanistic behavior in the elementary school classroom by focusing on their objectives, methods, materials, and evaluation measures. We have titled these strategies "Gestalt Game Approaches" and "Case Study Approaches."* We will also discuss techniques for extending these two approaches.

Since both of the strategies and the content with which they deal which we intend to describe are based on certain value judgments or commitments we hold to be "true," we wish to make such judgments clear at the onset:**

1. *Major problems facing citizens of our nation and other nations are humanistic subject-matter content for all curriculum areas in elementary schools.* This is not to say that the statement of the problem or the manner in which it is treated should be the same from classroom to classroom. It is to say that a problem such as pollution or environmental violence is legitimate subject matter for instruction in art, music, mathematics, science, physical education, language arts, social studies, reading, or any other category of the curriculum. Students in art may wish to express their feelings toward threats to the environment in a drawing or painting; students singing *America the Beautiful* should pause to reflect on the same theme; a math problem may focus on census figures describing the movement of people from the city to the suburbs, in part because of pollution; a science class may discuss the composition of a polluted body of water; students in physical education may take a hike to a polluted stream with an industrial complex on one side and a rural setting on the other; an essay or poetry may be the result of a language arts exposure to polluted air; and a student in reading or social studies may read a description of factory life during the early stages of industrialization in the United States or England.

---

*These approaches and related materials were developed as part of a University of North Carolina—Greensboro and University of Wisconsin–Milwaukee curriculum project. The authors of this book were actively involved in the building and testing of classroom materials. Directors of the project are Dale L. Brubaker and James B. Macdonald.

**Convictions of a more general nature are stated in Parts I and II. Value judgments specifically related to strategies for implementing humanistic education are the topic for the present discussion.

2. The flexibility of subject matter noted in the previous paragraph is based on a second value judgment on our part, namely, *the learning processes in which the student is engaged are more important than the particular substantive results of such processes.* Let us return to the problem of pollution to demonstrate this point. The student's conclusion (substantive result) with respect to a particular legislative bill in congress on the subject of pollution is less important than the student's acquiring a feeling for the pollution problem, learning analytic skills, and commiting himself to a course of action. Our point is that in every curriculum area the student should have a *feeling* for the subject matter involved, an *understanding* of working relationships in the curriculum area being studied, and a *commitment for involvement* on his own part. This is to say that his being actively engaged in that which he is learning is more important than the particular results of such engagement.

3. Our emphasis on the need for students to have a feeling for the problem involved is based on our belief that *the affective dimension of learning has too often been either neglected or misused on the part of elementary school teachers.* In cases where the affective dimension has been neglected, teachers have often emphasized structure, e.g., rote memory—at the expense of understanding. In cases where the affective dimension has been misused, teachers have often tried to achieve consensus by sermonizing—eliciting agreement as to predetermined conclusions—at the expense of inquiry.

In our judgment, elementary school students need to have (1) a feeling that a problem is important and (2) a feeling for more specific elements of the problem situation. For example, a fifth-grade student should not only feel that police-community confrontation in the inner city is a problem but should also feel empathy for both the police and members of the community. A white suburban pupil who draws a picture of what she would look like if she were black should not only have a feeling for the problem of being black in a predominantly white society but should also empathize with those who are prejudiced against because of their blackness and those who are prejudiced. In short, there should be role identification on her part for a better understanding of the problem situation.

Our emphasis on the feeling dimension does not by any means entail a rejection of the cognitive dimension of learning. Such emphasis is instead the result of our belief that new strategies for instruction that focus on affective learning need to be explored. This emphasis on affective dimensions of learning is basic to the strategies discussed in the following chapters. The strategies attempt to obtain an emotional commitment on the part of the learner by placing him in situations which enable him to experience emotions similar to those of people engaged in real-life social problems. This means that many of the teaching methods in the strategies utilize simulation materials or situations, particularly sociodrama or role playing and the use of case studies.

4. Another value judgment we have made is that *the working relationships in any area of the elementary school curriculum can best be understood when stated conceptually.* By *concept* we mean an abstracted quality common to diverse phenomena. For example, art, music, and other aesthetic forms can in part be understood as an expression of *ethnocentrism.* Our basic position is that once a learner understands a concept in one setting, he should be able to use it as a tool for understanding in other situations.

5. A fifth conviction we share is that *the teacher along with the pupils is a learner and searcher for understanding and for solutions to problems.* This is in contrast to the more typical situation in which the sermonizer, the person with predetermined conclusions, makes an emotional appeal in order to convince students of the validity of his biases. The teacher is expected to be a coordinator, catalyst, and learner rather than a more authoritarian moral judge and dispenser of knowledge. The role reversal discussed in Part II is an essential condition for a humanistic teaching-learning situation. The strategies encourage role reversal as well as extensive student-student communication of a verbal and nonverbal nature.

Now that we have identified major value judgments we hold as expressed in our strategies for humanistic instruction, we can proceed to detailed descriptions of the strategies themselves. Chapter 5 discusses Gestalt game strategies and humanistic content. Case study approaches are presented in Chapter 6. The last two chapters deal with extensions of these two approaches. Chapter 7 focuses on the study of knowledge problems and Chapter 8 presents and discusses techniques for social action.

Gestalt Game Approaches

Gestalt techniques are based on the premise that the physical, psychological, and biological are integrated rather than separated from each other. In using the label *Gestalt games,* we are simply referring to a series of experiences in the form of lesson plans we have devised, each of which is based on the Gestalt premise. The reader will find that the lesson plans described in this chapter are different from more traditional instructional approaches because they allow for many different kinds of emotional expression in the classrooms. In short, the affective being of the pupil as well as the cognitive is an important consideration for those who use Gestalt game approaches.*

As noted in the introduction to this section of the book, our discussion will focus on objectives, methods, materials, and evaluation.

Objectives

When referring to objectives, a useful distinction can be made between the philosophical and the technical. The philosophical dimension refers to the directions or goals that one feels should be pursued; the technical dimension refers to the manner in which goals can be stated most efficiently. The introduction to this section of the book spelled out the philosophical commitments or value orientation of the Gestalt games approach. It remains for us to treat the technical dimension of objectives.

---

*We have adopted the distinction between cognitive, affective, and psychomotor used by David R. Krathwohl, *et. al.* Cognitive objectives ". . . emphasize remembering or reproducing something which has presumably been learned" or "the solving of some intellective task for which the individual has to determine the essential problem and then reorder given material or combine it with ideas, methods, or procedures previously learned." Affective objectives ". . . emphasize a feeling tone, an emotion, or a degree of acceptance or rejection." Psychomotor objectives ". . . emphasize some muscular or motor skill, some manipulation of material and objects, or some act which requires a neuromuscular coordination." David Krathwohl, Benjamin S. Bloom, and Bertram B. Masia. *Taxonomy of Educational Objectives,* Vol. II, (New York: David McKay Co., 1956), pp. 6-7.

Behavioral and Nonbehavioral Objectives

In our judgment, instructional goals for Gestalt games should be stated behaviorally where possible. They communicate the purpose of each game more precisely than other forms of objectives.

Those who want to state all instructional goals in behavioral terms want a preciseness and clarity seldom found in traditional statements of objectives, however. They are reacting to vague terms such as *understanding* and *appreciation*. For example, Robert F. Mager, author of *Preparing Instructional Objectives*, criticizes the objective, "To develop an appreciation for music," for not stating exactly what it is that the learner *does* to demonstrate he has achieved the objective. Mager suggests that the teacher who states an "appreciation" objective such as the one mentioned above would have to accept any of the following behaviors as evidence that the learner has reached the objective.

1. The learner sighs in ecstasy when listening to Bach.
2. The learner buys a hi-fi system and $500 worth of records.
3. The learner correctly answers 95 multiple-choice questions on the history of music.
4. The learner writes an eloquent essay on the meaning of 37 operas.
5. The learner says, "oh man, this is the most. It's just *too* much."[1]

Furthermore, Mager adds that he does not criticize the worthiness of the goal, "To develop an appreciation for music," but instead feels the objective's vagueness fails to communicate. In fact, Mager does criticize the worthiness of the "appreciation" objective by excluding it as a stated objective. It is true that many objectives should be stated behaviorally for we can then evaluate more easily the learner's progress toward such objectives. However, learning involves much more than that which can be evaluated. For example, imagine for a moment that you are a sixth-grade student in a class that has just studied Napoleon. You are listening to a Napoleonic march the teacher is playing on the record-player. You know that there is interaction between your mind, feelings, and the Napoleonic march. Yet you wish to remain silent and simply let yourself experience listening to the march. You do not want to talk about the march or take a test to give the teacher information about your ideas and feelings. Your experience is very personal and important to you. A behavioral statement of objectives concerning your experience would miss the mark. In fact, it could be dysfunctional—especially in the event that the teacher interfered with or blocked communication between you and the recording by using behavioral measures. We will refer to this as the existential argument against stating *all* objectives in behavioral terms.

The existential argument is especially relevant to the humanities element of the elementary school curriculum, for the humanities have many nonscientific affective objectives. These objectives often do not lend themselves to behavioral evaluation. As we consider the humanities to be a very important part of a humanistic curriculum, the implications for leaving room for nonbehavioral objectives or using a general form of behavioral objectives are obvious. Behavioral or other objectives that restrict student interests and self-direction violate humanism. The objectives stated for Gestalt games should be viewed as *possible* objectives. Many other and often more worthy objectives develop as the games are in progress, and these objectives which emanate from both the students and the teacher should be pursued.

Focusing Our Objectives

Objectives may focus on the teacher, the topic or subject matter, and the pupil. That is, we may center our attention on *what the teacher aims to teach, the content or subject matter,* or *what the student is expected to learn.* The following objectives, each of which has a different focus, demonstrate ways in which objectives can be written.

Focus on Teacher	*Focus on Content or Subject Matter*	*Focus on Student*
1. Teaches that pollution is a threat to our environment.	1. Pollution as a threat to our environment.	1. Learns that pollution is a threat to our environment.
2. Teaches analytic skills.	2. Analytic skills.	2. Learns analytic skills.
3. Teaches students to identify Mona Lisa.	3. Identification of Mona Lisa.	3. Learns to identify Mona Lisa.

In the following paragraphs we will state the case for focusing objectives on teacher, topic, and student, and then present our own position, namely, that primary attention should be given to student-focused goals but not to the exclusion of teacher and subject-matter goals. Our case rests to a large extent on expanding the definition of *learner* to include both student and teacher.

1. *Goals should be teacher centered.* To focus our objectives on the student and/or subject matter to the exclusion of the teacher is a mistake. The humanistic teacher is every bit as much a learner in the educational process as is the student. If we believe the rhetoric that the

teacher's example as a learner is contagious, then it follows that many goals should be teacher centered.

To center our attention on the teacher's learning is different than focusing on what the teacher wants his students to learn. The teacher may talk about a subject such as the population explosion without his students learning about the population explosion. It is also true that students learn more than we intend for them to learn. For example, students learn something about political trade-offs by giving the teacher affection in return for good grades even though the teacher may not know that such knowledge has been acquired. Therefore, to center our attention on what the teacher learns or what the student learns is different than focusing on what the teacher wants the students to learn or for that matter what the student wants the teacher to learn.

The following is an example of a teacher-centered goal that defines the teacher as learner: Throughout a unit on air pollution, the teacher should attempt to treat his "pet" solution—industries should not distribute profits to stockholders until they have greatly minimized the emission of pollutants into the air—as one among many proposals for minimizing air pollution. This treatment of the subject of air pollution on the part of the teacher would be evident in his classroom actions, for students would be exposed to a variety of possible solutions. Students should be able to decide what solution they personally support, and the teacher should demonstrate that he will take a different position than the one he presently holds when given better evidence to the contrary. (For example, in one classroom the teacher initially felt the best solution to air pollution was government subsidies in the form of "tax breaks" but a student countered by attempting to convince her that this meant taxpayers could end up paying for pollution they did not create.) The teacher openly adopted the student's position that industries should apply profits toward pollution control rather than return such profits to stockholders. Whether the sixth-grade teacher was right or wrong is not as important for our purposes of discussion as the fact that the teacher behaved as if her ideas were subject to revision in the public forum—the classroom.

2. *Goals should be content or subject matter centered.* Teachers tend to behave on the basis of one of two major views of subject matter: (1) subject matter is a static body of knowledge to be transmitted to the student; and (2) subject matter is proximate and always is in the process of being revised. The former view is often supported by those who believe that discovery of and addition to subject matter for the elementary school rests in the hands of experts, usually located at universities. The latter view is often supported by those who feel that the

teacher and his students play an important part in discovering and revising subject matter. The latter view is a rationale for focusing our objectives on the discovery and revision of subject matter as well as focusing on the teacher and pupil.

Recent emphasis on structure and asking the kinds of questions asked by academicians in the various disciplines lend support to the second view of subject matter—that the learner (teacher or student) is an active participant in discovering and revising subject matter. Jerome S. Bruner, a Harvard University psychologist, argues in the following manner.

> What a scientist does at his desk or in his laboratory, what a literary critic does in reading a poem, are of the same order as what anybody does when he is engaged in like activities—if he is to achieve understanding. The difference is in degree, not in kind. The schoolboy learning physics *is* a physicist, and it is easier for him to learn physics behaving like a physicist than doing something else.[2]

A second reason for arguing that the learner is an active participant in discovering and revising subject matter is based on the information explosion. We are told that the amount of information available to the literate world doubles each fifteen years or so.[3] As the amount of information available (subject matter) increases, the relativity or subjectivity of choice of information for instructional purposes also increases. Therefore, the learner as inquirer should have a more important role in content or subject-matter selection.

The following is an example of an objective that takes into account the tentativeness of subject matter while at the same time focusing on subject matter: The students in my fifth-grade social studies class studying American history should demonstrate that they question the physiographical thesis (the physical geography of the United States was primary in shaping the American) by reading and discussing a case study arguing that the industrialization of the United States was primary in shaping the American. (Students in the fifth-grade class would probably not use the terms stated in the objective but could nevertheless deal with the subject matter in their own terms while retaining the meaning stated in the objective.)

3. *Goals should be student centered.* Some educators would have us focus our objectives on the student to the exclusion of the teacher and subject matter. After all, they would argue, education is for the student. We agree that *the primary focus* of objectives in elementary school should be on the student, but not to the exclusion of the teacher and subject matter. It is our view that the learning process is a constant interaction between teacher, student, and subject matter—interaction in which all parties to the process are subject to change. We have used

the phrase *subject to change* rather than *change* for two reasons: (1) change may be overt, covert, potential, or nonexistent, although in each case those interested in the process have been exposed to the educational process; and (2) it is improbable, if not impossible, to know all of the effects of the educational process on those interested in the process from moment to moment.

In summary, objectives in the strategy we have identified as Gestalt game approaches (1) are stated in general behavioral terms where possible although not to the exclusion of nonbehavioral objectives, and (2) focus primarily on the student although not to the exclusion of the teacher and subject matter.

Methods

Methods are the processes students and teachers go through in attempting to reach learning objectives. In short, they are the vehicle adopted for achieving one's goals. All of the methods adopted in the Gestalt game strategies are simulative in nature for the learner is placed in situations which enable him to experience thoughts, values, and emotions similar to those of people engaged in real-life social problems. The real-life social problems and social accomplishments with which the games deal are humanistic content or subject matter. They are humanistic because they focus on man and his achievements and failures, his joys and his sorrows, his aspirations and fears. The games also facilitate humanism because the type of discussion and action that results from the simulative situation meets the requirements of humanistic teacher and student behavior. The games establish situations from which humanistic behavior seems to naturally flow. Because of this commitment to simulation techniques, we have placed particular stress on the methods of sociodrama and role playing. (The terms are often used synonymously.) One advantage of role playing, as mentioned above, is that the pupil plays a role other than that of himself, thus empathizing with others. A second advantage is that the participant acts spontaneously in response to others' actions in much the same way as he must do in life outside the school.[4]

What is involved in the role-playing method? Fannie Shaftel, in her book *Role-Playing for Social Values,* describes the processes involved: "Role-playing focuses upon handling data . . . , tentative decision-making in the choosing among alternatives, experiencing consequences . . . , and making final decisions. . . ."[5] The following lesson for upper elementary school students demonstrates the role-playing method.

Lesson Plan 1: Landlord-Tenant Confrontation (Intergroup Relations)

OBJECTIVES: As a result of this lesson, students may conclude that:
1. A given action or event has many causes.
2. People concerned with an event interpret what occurs according to their own priority of values (belief systems).
3. People who wish to influence the outcome of an event behave on the basis of their own priority of values.
4. Landlords commonly have a different priority of values than do tenants.

METHODS AND MATERIALS:
1. Announce to the class that a landlord has just asked his financially poor tenant's family to leave their apartment. The class' task is to identify reasons that this confrontation has occurred. Tell them that two students can act out the meeting between the landlord and tenant, and by viewing this scene the class may be able to estimate why this event happened.
2. Select one volunteer to play the role of landlord. Hand him a card labeled *Landlord* citing some reasons for why he is evicting the tenants. Tell him that he should add other reasons as well.
3. Select another volunteer to play the role of tenant. Hand him a card labeled *Tenant* citing some reasons he has not paid the rent. He can also think of other reasons.
4. Before the role-playing begins, suggest that each student mentally or actually divide a sheet of paper into two columns, one titled *Landlord* and the other *Tenant*. As the scene is acted out, they are to record the reasons for the actions of the two characters.
5. Have the two actors come before the class and describe the setting somewhat in this fashion: "We'll imagine that the landlord has just knocked on the door of the tenant's apartment. When the tenant opens it, the landlord steps in and says that the family will have to move. When the tenant asks why, the landlord starts to give his reasons. Then the tenant answers back. Now, let's begin with the landlord knocking on the door."
6. When the sociodrama has gone far enough to elicit a variety of reasons or arguments on both sides, ask the two characters to switch roles and play the scene again.
7. After the second playing of the scene, conduct a discussion of the event focusing on individual viewpoints, values, and feelings in regard to the event, its causes, and its solution.

EVALUATION:
Observe student responses in the role playing and discussion. Using a controversial event from the newspaper, hold another discussion on why the event may have occurred. More than one cause should be proposed.

In the preceding lesson, the roles of the landlord and tenant were apparent to the class from the beginning. In the following lesson plan, the class is asked to identify what the participants are doing—their roles. Only the participants or actors are informed by the teacher as to their roles. In this way the role-playing method invites the class to evaluate how well the participants are playing their roles.

Lesson Plan 2: Comparing Cultures (Intergroup Relations)

OBJECTIVES: As a result of this lesson, the students should be able to:
1. Identify some basic tasks common to all people.
2. Describe what is meant by the *culture* of a particular society.
3. Compare and contrast briefly the culture of a given society with their own culture.

METHODS AND MATERIALS:
1. Choose three volunteers to go to the front of the room. Tell the three students that they are to pretend they are eating. Give one student chopsticks, the second silverware, and the third nothing. Instruct the student with the chopsticks to pretend he is eating rice and seaweed, the student with the silverware to pretend he is eating roast beef, and the third student with no utensils to pretend he is eating whale blubber.
2. Ask the class a series of questions concerning what the three students are doing. Once they have identified the common task—eating—ask more specific questions as to what cultures or societies use such implements. Help the students discover the conclusion that although all of the students are performing the same task, the way in which this task is performed varies from society to society and culture to culture.
3. Choose three different volunteers to role play. Instruct the three students that they are going to use different methods to seek food. Give one student a fishing net, the second a makeshift spear, and the third a shopping list.
4. Ask questions similar to the ones asked previously. Have the students discover the conclusion that although all people seek food, they fulfill this need in different ways from society to society and culture to culture.
5. Show the class a picture of an Eskimo family outside of their house and have the students compare their own housing conditions with those of the Eskimos. Have the students discover that all men have a basic need for shelter although they meet this need in different ways in different societies and cultures.
6. Discuss what is meant by the term *culture*.
7. An alternative procedure to using a role play-discuss-role play-discuss sequence is to do all of the role playing first and then have one lengthy discussion.

EVALUATION:
Have the students list four basic tasks common to all people. Then read an account of the kind of education an Eskimo child acquires. Ask the students for a verbal comparison of this education to their own. Ask the students to compare other aspects of Eskimo culture to their own.

In the first two examples of the role-playing method, the students directly involved in playing roles were given very specific information as to the subject-matter content of the role. If the actors had had no experience in playing the roles, they still could have played the roles because of prescribed content. In the following lesson, students are asked to draw on their own experience—affective and cognitive—in order to play the roles.

Lesson Plan 3: Confrontation with Someone You Dislike (Intergroup Relations)

OBJECTIVES: The following experiences should enable students to:
1. Identify a national figure they dislike.
2. Relate the emotional feelings they have toward this person as well as the reasons for such feelings.
3. Play the role of this national figure in order to empathize with him.
4. Draw the conclusion that feelings of dislike as identified in relation to national figures may be similar to feelings of dislike for those in their more immediate environment, and feeling empathy for such people usually reduces the amount of conflict between hostile parties.

METHODS AND MATERIALS:
1. Have students form several small groups—5 students per group—with each group sitting in a circle. Place an empty chair in the middle of each circle.
2. Ask the students to begin discussing some national figure they have seen on television, heard on the radio, read about, or heard of through conversations with other people. (This national figure may be a recording artist, artist, politician, or member of any other profession. It should be *anyone* who has caught their attention.)
3. Ask the students to limit their discussion to those national figures who make them angry—someone they dislike.
4. Ask a student from each circle who seems to be quite emotionally involved to pretend that the empty chair in the center of the circle is the person they have identified. Have any students in the circle who share feelings of dislike openly confront the "target" with their views.

5. After they have vented their feelings, have "hostile" students play the role of the "target" and respond to their previously-made criticisms.
6. Ask other students in the circle to stand behind the "hostile" chair or "target" chair and enter into the confrontation.
7. Have each student in the room face an empty chair and replay a situation in which they recently confronted someone toward whom they were angry. Then have each student sit in the empty chair and respond to their criticism.
8. Discuss the role-playing incidents and the empathy the students felt.

EVALUATION:

Have each student write a few sentences in which he describes how he felt in the role of someone he had previously criticized. Write the conclusion stated in objective 4 on the board and determine whether students agree or disagree with the statement. Discuss reasons for students' views.

An even more open-ended role-playing situation would be the following: Have students write and present a brief skit on the subject WHAT POLLUTION MEANS TO ME.

In summary, role playing or sociodrama is the primary *method* used in Gestalt game approaches. Role definition may be viewed on a continuum from tightly prescribed to open-ended. This method facilitates humanism because the content of the games is humanistic content and the behavior of the teacher and students during and following the game that results from this approach often meets the criteria of humanistic classroom behavior.

Materials

The Gestalt game approaches strategy includes materials consistent with the role-playing or sociodrama methodology. The materials we have built to implement the Gestalt game strategy consist of lesson plans organized around humanistic themes (such as Urbanization) and around humanistic problems or accomplishments subsumed under themes (such as Noninvolvement with Others' Lives or Art in the City). The rationale for including both themes and problems is that the problems' approach when used singly tends to emphasize the negative aspect of human relations while overlooking that "which goes right" among people and between people and their environment. A thematic approach leaves room and calls attention to both the cement that holds things together and difficulties or problems that must be solved in order to keep the structure together. Our emphasis on themes and problems demonstrates our value judgment that we should work within the structure or "establishment" in order to achieve a more humanistic world. This is another way of saying that we oppose an idealism that overlooks problems and a cynicism that overlooks man's accomplishments.

Each lesson plan we have built involves three elements designed to promote more humanistic instruction: (1) a possible problem to be solved; (2) possible concepts to extract or comprehend; and (3) a social setting. The structure in Table V demonstrates our plan. It identifies five major humanistic themes and numerous humanistic problems and accomplishments. Each of the twelve lesson plans presented in this chapter deals with one of these problems or accomplishments.*

TABLE V

CURRICULUM STRUCTURE
HUMANISTIC THEMES, PROBLEMS, AND ACCOMPLISHMENTS

THEMES—*Sample Lesson Titles*
(+ = Lesson centers on accomplishments)
(− = Lesson centers on problems)

I. *URBANIZATION*
   + Loyalty to community
   + City knowledge, rural knowledge
   + Back to nature
   + Art in the city
   − Noninvolvement with others' lives
   − Commuter attitudes
   − Trouble in schools

II. *TECHNOLOGICAL CHANGE*
   + Information: Storage and retrieval
   + Influencing the media
   + Use of leisure time
   + Vocations
   − Traffic
   − Dehumanization
   − Technological unemployment
   − Vocations: Poverty

III. *SURVIVAL*
   + Recycling cans and papers
   + Information summarizing
   + Compromising 1
   − Overcrowded territory
   − Air pollution
   − Noise pollution

*Additional Gestalt games are contained in the Appendix.

IV. *INTERGROUP RELATIONS—HUMAN INTERACTION*
   + Verbal-Nonverbal communication
   + Positive reinforcers: Smiles and nods
   + Positive reinforcers: Comments
   + Facts and values
   + Compromising 2
   + Feeling black or white
   + Comparing cultures
   + Diplomacy
   − Ethnic stereotypes
   − Landlord-tenant confrontation
   − White police in a black ghetto
   − Informers in society
   − Preferential treatment
   − Confrontation with someone you dislike
V. *INTRAGROUP RELATIONS*
   + Respecting the rights of others
   + Compromise 3
   − Intolerance
   − Marginality: Immigrants vs. Anglo-Saxon Americans
   − Marginality: Parents vs. peers
   − Marginality: Male and female roles
   − Conformity

As one of the basic tenets of humanistic instruction is the integration of the cognitive and the affective, it is necessary to spell out in greater detail exactly how the games achieve such integration. The affective dimension is clearly achieved in each lesson plan designed to evoke emotional insights. Lesson plans 1 and 3 focus on volatile situations involving confrontation between two, often hostile, parties. The lessons simulate real-life situations that occur daily in our nation. Lesson plan 2 is somewhat less emotionally charged. At the same time an appeal is made to the child's senses in having him use utensils for eating, objects for acquiring food, and a picture describing shelter in the Eskimo culture.

The cognitive dimension of the Gestalt game strategy is indicated in problem-solving processes and concepts. The following lesson plan demonstrates one aspect of problem-solving that we have judged important for students to learn, namely, the recognition of the distinction between factual claims and value claims.

Lesson Plan 4: Facts and Values (Intergroup Relations)

OBJECTIVES: On an evaluation sheet, students should demonstrate their recognition of the distinction between factual claims and value claims by:
   1. Writing F in front of factual statements and VC in front of value claims.

2. Underline words which help identify value claims, like *good, bad, better, best.*

METHODS AND MATERIALS:
1. Hand the students a sheet containing the following material:

....
    A. Look at the pictures of the two football players.
       Player Number 1 is named ....
       Player Number 2 is named ....
       Who is the better football player? ....
       Why is he better? ....
    B. Look at the pictures of the two actors.
       Actor Number 3 is named ....
       Actor Number 4 is named ....
       Who is the better actor? ....
       Why is he better? ....
    C. Look at the pictures of the two actresses.
       Actress Number 5 is named ....
       Actress Number 6 is named ....
       Who is the better actress? ....
       Why is she better? ....
    D. Write *F* in front of *facts*. Write *VC* in front of *values or opinions.*
       .... Diahann Carroll is a television actress.
       .... Jim Brown was a football player who became an actor.
       .... Harry Belafonte is a singer.
       .... Jim Brown is a better actor than Harry Belafonte.
       .... Gail Fisher is a better singer than Diahann Carroll.
       .... O. J. Simpson cannot dance as well as Harry Belafonte.
       .... Diahann Carroll and Gail Fisher have both been on television.
....

2. Hold up a picture of Jim Brown and place it on the blackboard chalk tray below a number *1*. Hold up a picture of O. J. Simpson and place it below number *2*. Ask the students to write answers to the questions under *A* on the worksheet. When they answer "Why is he better?" write some of their oral responses on the chalkboard.
3. Follow the same procedure in having them fill out section *B*, using photographs of Jim Brown as an actor and Harry Belafonte. Do the same for section *C* with photographs of Diahann Carroll and Gail Fisher.
4. Ask whether they can tell which statements under A, B, and C are facts and which are opinions or values. If they cannot make this distinction, explain the differences between facts and value claims.

5. When all student questions have been answered, have each student complete section D on his own. Then ask them to underline each word in a value claim that helped him decide it was an opinion.
   6. Discuss with the class the correct answers to the statements and questions.

Other problem-solving processes emphasized in lesson plans include formulating hypotheses, gathering and weighing the validity of data, tendering proximate conclusions, and committing oneself to a course of action.

The conceptual nature of each lesson plan is also cognitive in orientation. Lesson plan 1, for example, was designed in part to familiarize students with the concept *multiple-causation* (objective 1) and lesson plan 3 focused on the concept of *culture.* The following lesson plan treats the concept *stereotype* by giving preferential treatment to one segment of an elementary school class.

Lesson Plan 5: Preferential Treatment (Intergroup Relations)
OBJECTIVES: As a result of this lesson, students should be able to:
   1. Develop a working definition of *stereotype,* such as, "What you think a person is like just from seeing him or hearing what group he belongs to."
   2. Define or cite examples of *preferential treatment.*
   3. Describe the feelings frequently experienced by people who enjoy preferential treatment (pleasure, a desire to retain preferred status, a psychological distance from those not accorded such treatment, guilt) and by those who do not (anger, puzzlement, loneliness, rejection).
   4. State advantages of stereotypes (such as easy to decide how to treat a person) and their disadvantages (such as you may treat a person in an unfair or harmful way).

METHODS AND MATERIALS:
   1. Have the class divide into two groups according to some physical characteristic, such as those who wear glasses versus those who do not (or those with blue eyes versus those with eyes of different colors, those with dark hair versus those with light, those who are taller versus those who are shorter). Tell the students the basis for the division, and move those with one characteristic, like those who wear glasses, to the desks on the right side of the room, and the rest of the students to the desks on the left side. Do not inform them of how this division will be used.
   2. Distribute ditto sheets or poetry or math puzzles to each group. The sheets given to the people with glasses are very legible. Those given to the group without glasses are nearly illegible.

3. Explain the sheet assignment to the entire class, but accept questions from and give explanations to only the group with glasses. If the students without glasses ask questions or complain about the illegible sheets, tell them: "Just do your work. Get busy and no complaints." If pupils wearing glasses ask questions, give them clear, pleasant answers.
4. As the students begin work, circulate among the students wearing glasses, helping them complete their work. Ignore the no-glasses students, except to discipline those who talk or are unruly.
5. Since the students wearing glasses will finish first, give them five or ten minutes of free time to chat and have a good time. If the no-glasses children finish early, tell them to check over their answers or get to work on arithmetic problems.
6. Following the brief recess of the students wearing glasses, conduct a general class discussion about what happened, how students felt, and why. Have a student volunteer write the opinions on the chalkboard under the categories *Haves* (for the students wearing glasses) and *Have-Nots* (for the no-glasses group).
7. Discuss what *stereotype* means. If no one knows, give a simple definition and ask students for some examples of stereotypes (based on skin color, church affiliation, age, sex, hair style.) Give additional examples of your own. Explain that some of them were receiving *preferential treatment* for a physical characteristic rather than on the basis of their personal behavior. Ask for other examples of people receiving preferential treatment for some group characteristic.
8. Discuss whether stereotypes are ever useful. Are they ever harmful? If students cannot cite examples, give some of your own.

EVALUATION:
Observation of students' responses during the discussion.

Earlier in this section of the book we indicated that in our view humanistic content is not limited to any subject-matter discipline. If the reader reexamines the themes, problems, and accomplishments cited in our overall plan, he will find implicit in them the assumption that humanistic content permeates the elementary school curriculum. At the same time, we feel that teachers should be given suggestions as to how the materials can be adjusted from class to class and subject-matter area to subject-matter area.

Adjusting Gestalt Game Lesson Plans

Racial tension in an inner city school was heightened by a series of confrontations between the city police, predominantly white, and the predominantly black community. One reason for the tension was the use of blacks to inform on blacks. (At this particular time ministers in the community were especially distrusted by many blacks who felt that such clergymen were informers.) The confrontation was naturally the subject matter for all classes during this period of time. Police were moved into the halls of schools for several days. An elementary school teacher used "language arts time" to try out the following lesson plans. She wanted her black students to discuss the feelings of blacks toward informers while at the same time understanding some of the feelings of white policemen in a black community during a time of crisis.

Lesson Plan 6: Informers in Society (Intergroup Relations)
OBJECTIVES: As a result of this lesson, students will be able to identify:
1. Feelings many blacks harbor toward police and toward others in their own group because police solicit blacks to inform on activities of their fellow community members (feelings of fear, hostility, social distance, or alienation).
2. Advantages and disadvantages of informers for the work of police and for the welfare of the individual who lives in the black community.

METHODS AND MATERIALS:
1. Explain to the class that one reason for conflict between the police and such groups as blacks living in urban centers is the use of black informers to get information about other blacks. Say that you are going to play a game to help the class identify and understand what feelings might arise in a group because of informers.
2. Have each student write his own name on a slip of paper. Collect the slips and redistribute them giving each student someone else's name. Tell the students not to let anyone know whose name they have. However, this name identifies the student who is their target. For the next ten minutes, each child is to watch his target so as to gather mental notes that would be useful in telling what the person looks like, what his habits are, and how he is likely to act. He should collect this information without the target child realizing who is watching him.
3. Permit students to follow their own interests in the classroom for ten minutes, moving wherever they desire.
4. After the period of free movement, conduct a general discussion. Either you or a student can function as a policeman who asks each informer what information he has collected about the target individual.
5. When a variety of informers' descriptions have been collected, discuss with class members what it felt like to be "spied on." List responses on the chalkboard.
6. Discuss advantages and disadvantages of using black informers to the police and to the black community. List these on the chalkboard.

GESTALT GAME APPROACHES 105

7. Discuss other situations in which informers are used (in school, in business organizations where people vie for promotion, on teams involving competition for positions).

EVALUATION:
Observe students' responses during the discussion.

Lesson Plan 7: Authority Representative in Hostile Group (Intergroup Relations)

OBJECTIVES: As a result of this lesson, students should be able to:
1. Identify the feelings that might be experienced by an authority figure, like a white policeman, in a hostile or fearful group, like the society of a black neighborhood. The feelings might include self-consciousness, loneliness, fear, anger, and hostility toward the group.
2. Suggest ways that barriers between the authority figure and the group might be reduced.

METHODS AND MATERIALS:
1. Explain to the class that they are going to act out a spontaneous play. Ask one volunteer to leave the room. Before he goes out, hand him a card explaining that he is a white policeman assigned to a black neighborhood. Some other policemen have told him the people in the neighborhood cannot be trusted and that they hate policemen.
2. While the policeman is out of the room, tell the class that they are blacks living in a neighborhood that has no whites. A new policeman has been assigned to their area. You hear that he is tough and he has been sent to arrest, or maybe beat up, as many blacks as he can. He is just waiting to accuse someone of doing something illegal. When the policeman returns to the room, the students are free to move around, but they should always keep a watch out for the policeman as they go about their business.
3. Bring the policeman back, and explain that everyone is free to do what he likes for the next ten minutes but not to leave the room.
4. After the ten minutes of freedom, ask the policeman how he feels. What did he experience? How did the rest of the class feel about him and about themselves? Note the responses on the chalkboard.
5. Discuss other instances in which an individual is in a strange or hostile group. If no suggestions are given, give your own examples (immigrant new to the country and does not speak the language well; a new child who comes to school in the middle of the year; an older adult among young people who consider him "a drag").
6. Discuss what might be done to improve the feelings between the white policeman in the black neighborhood.

EVALUATION:
Have each student write about a situation in which he was in a strange group and about how he felt. Have him indicate whether he was a representative of outside authority when he was in the group.

Another less tense problem situation prompted a teacher to adjust the previous lesson plans (6 and 7) to his needs. His fifth-grade students read about immigration but had little feeling for what it was like to be an immigrant. He adjusted the lesson plan in the following way and used it primarily as a lesson in social studies.

Lesson Plan 8: Immigrants vs. Anglo-Saxon Americans (Intragroup Relations)

OBJECTIVES: As a result of this lesson, students should be able to:
1. Identify some of the feelings that might be experienced by an immigrant after his arrival in a new country. The feelings might include self-consciousness, loneliness, fear, rejection, anger, and hostility.
2. Express by analogy their view that immigrants in the United States had similar feelings.
3. Suggest ways that barriers between immigrants and Anglo-Saxon Americans might have been reduced and ways they might be reduced today.

METHODS AND MATERIALS:
1. Explain to students that the immigrants are from the economically distressed parts of Southern Europe and Ireland. They have a language difficulty, live on "the other side of the tracks" and are predominantly of the Roman Catholic faith. They work for low wages in the local factories. Some are affiliated with a radical labor organization, the International Workers of the World. (Explain to students that these introductory statements are background for a game they will now play.)
2. Ask each student to write his name on a piece of paper. Collect and mix the papers and then hand each student a paper with a name (not his own) on it.
3. Have each student stand up and give *his own* real name so that the student who holds the name of his classmate can identify his target. The target is to be viewed as an immigrant.
4. Ask each student to observe and take mental notes on what would be useful information in describing the target's behavior. Have students mill around the room for approximately five minutes.
5. Inform the students that you, the teacher, are a Pinkerton detective and ask each student for information that might be useful in describing the target's behavior.
6. Using a tape recorder, interview each student for a few minutes asking him his reaction to being watched.
7. Through discussion draw analogy to original background information about immigrants and have students suggest ways in which barriers could have been reduced and still can be reduced.

A fourth-grade teacher had arranged for a day-long student exchange between an inner-city school and her own suburban school. During the day, three black poets from the inner-city school read their poetry. It was apparent to the suburban teacher that her fourth graders had little feeling for what it meant to be black. Therefore, on the following day, she used "language arts time" to try out the following Gestalt game:

Lesson Plan 9: Feeling Black (Intergroup Relations)
OBJECTIVES: As a result of this experience students should be able to:
1. Identify many of their own feelings toward blacks.
2. Express reasons why their own "white background" makes it difficult to imagine what it must be like to be black.
3. Create a working definition of the concept *stereotype*.

METHODS AND MATERIALS:
1. Say to your students: "Close your eyes for a few minutes and imagine yourself in front of a large mirror." (Three minutes of silence to think about this.)
2. Then say, "Look very carefully in the mirror at your face. Notice your eyes, nose, and lips, your chin, eyebrows, and hair. Concentrate on your face." (Three minutes of silence to think about this.)
3. Then say, "As you look in the mirror, you notice that your face is black." (Three minutes to think about this.)
4. Ask the students to open their eyes and discuss what they experienced. List common responses on board.
5. Discuss with students why they thought they felt the way they did. (Also why it was difficult for some to imagine.)
6. Introduce the term *stereotype* and discuss advantages and disadvantages in using stereotypes.

EVALUATION:
Students' verbal responses and physical reactions while playing the game.

Another elementary school teacher in the same building heard about the game and decided to adjust it to her own needs. With the same objectives in mind, she asked her students during "art time" to draw self-portraits imagining themselves to be black rather than white. Students then discussed what they had drawn. (One obstacle to the use of Gestalt games is demonstrated in an incident that occurred because of this art assignment. One girl did not have time to finish her drawing in school and asked if she could take it home to complete it. While completing it at home on the kitchen table, her father saw the picture and ripped it into pieces. The girl told her teacher about the incident with tears in her eyes. In this case, however, the parents did not contact the school.)

Gestalt games cannot only be adjusted from subject area to subject area, but also from grade level to grade level. The following lesson plan, for example, was used in third-grade and sixth-grade classes.

Lesson Plan 10: Overcrowded Territory (Survival)
OBJECTIVES: As a result of this lesson students should be able to:
1. Identify some of the results of increased numbers of people residing in a limited space, such as frustration, hostility often resulting in physical violence, self-consciousness, and a feeling of despair.

METHODS AND MATERIALS:
1. Act as if you are conducting a regular 30 minute session throughout this game.
2. Mark off an area in the rear of the room with enough space for 4 chairs jammed together.
3. Assign two volunteers to the area. (If third graders, ask these two students to try to remember their feelings for the remainder of the game. If sixth graders, ask these two students to keep a diary with brief descriptive sentences telling how they feel at a particular time: for example, 2:10—I feel away from the group; 2:25—I'm thirsty.)
4. Add another student to the space every 3 or 4 minutes so that you end up with 7 or 8 people in the space. (Students will be forced to remove the chairs and will finish the game standing close together.)
5. Ask the two original students to recall what happened (third grade) or read their diaries (sixth grade). Then ask other students in the area to tell what they felt. (Have students relate their feelings while still in the crowded space.)
6. Show the students pictures of people in the United States and world that demonstrate crowded living conditions. Discuss how they must feel in such an environment.

EVALUATION:
Students' verbal responses and/or diaries.

A second example of a lesson plan that can be adjusted focuses on a first-grade class and a third-grade class.

Lesson Plan 11: Vocations (Technological Change)
OBJECTIVES: As a result of this lesson, students should be able to explain how the following factors can influence a person's choice of a vocation:
1. Whether he works inside or outside.
2. The amount of money the job pays.
3. The amount and kind of education required.
4. The opinion of others (family, friends) about how desirable the job is (the status of the occupation).

METHODS AND MATERIALS:
1. Say to the class, "Your fathers and mothers, your uncles and aunts, and your older brothers and sisters have jobs to earn money. Other grown-up people around the neighborhood here have jobs, too. Could you name some of these jobs or kinds of work?"
2. Write students' suggestions on the blackboard. If range of occupations is not voluntarily given, stimulate suggestions with suggestions of your own.
3. Choose four jobs from the list you have written on the board and place each at the top of a column on the blackboard, as follows:

   nurse   *doctor*   *mailman*   *switchboard operator*

4. Discuss why people would choose such jobs. Feature the four variables in the objectives and any others that arise in filling the column, such as:

1st grade class

nurse	*doctor*	*mailman*	*switchboard operator*
usually works inside	usually works inside	usually works outside	usually works inside
average salary	high salary	average salary	low to average salary
a few years after high school	a lot of years after high school	learn on job after high school	learn on job after high school
a good job for a girl	like this job very much	good job for man	good job for a girl

3rd grade class

nurse	*doctor*	*mailman*	*switchboard operator*
usually works inside	usually works inside	usually works outside	usually works inside
about $7,000	about $20,000	about $8,000	about $5,000
usually 2 years education beyond high school	usually 8 years beyond high school	education on job (trained on job after high school)	trained on job after high school

EVALUATION:
List jobs of people in the school—teacher, principal, secretary, bus driver, custodian. Discuss each job in terms of four variables listed above.

In summary, the Gestalt game strategy that we have developed includes materials mainly in the form of easily adjustable lesson plans. These lesson plans focus on problems to be solved, concepts to be comprehended, and a social setting. Minor alterations can be made in each lesson plan to account for subject-matter areas and grade level. Also, teachers can easily create their own games to either fit the structure presented in Table V or to develop other themes. The game strategy represents an effective technique to begin to create humanistic instruction.

Evaluation

Thus far in this chapter we have discussed Gestalt game approaches in terms of objectives, methods, and materials. We now turn to the matter of evaluation—the procedure by which we see how close we have come to our goals.

Many of the objectives for each lesson plan were stated in behavioral terms, thus making the task of evaluation of student progress much easier. The teacher knows what kinds of student behavior or actions will serve as evidence that the students have reached the goals.

The evaluation measures in each lesson plan rely heavily on verbal responses although on occasion students are expected to write brief essays or fill in short written answers. Many of the lesson plans also emphasize nonverbal physical reactions to controversial situations. The teacher is expected to take mental notes of such actions thus providing him with another method of evaluation. The following lesson plan demonstrates the importance of evaluating nonverbal actions.

Lesson Plan 12: Verbal-Nonverbal Communication (Intergroup Relations)

OBJECTIVES: As a result of this lesson, students should demonstrate that they can identify and discuss the following generalizations:
1. Communication (expressing your thoughts so that others understand you and in turn understanding their expression of thoughts) depends on:
    a. the words one uses
    b. body movement, for example, gestures and posture
    c. eye contact
    d. attitudes of participants, for example, desire of participants to convey ideas

GESTALT GAME APPROACHES 111

2. When people talk to each other they often change what they heard or leave out part of what they have heard so that different meaning is conveyed.

METHODS AND MATERIALS:
1. Have students pair off and place their chairs back to back. Then say, "Sit straight, be very quiet, and don't turn your head. Think of the person behind you. Try to tell him something without talking." Then ask the question, "Did you understand what he was trying to tell you? Why?" (Students will probably say they couldn't see or hear the person.)
2. Give the following instructions: "Sit straight, don't turn your head, but try to talk to the person behind you." Then say, "Did you understand what he was trying to tell you? Why?" (Students will probably say that they had to shout and even then didn't communicate very well.)
3. Then say, "Now stand up, face each other, close your eyes, and talk to each other." In a few minutes add, "Did you understand what he tried to tell you? Was it still somewhat difficult? Why?" (Students will probably say they could not see the other person.)
4. Finally, say: "Now still remain standing and talk to each other with your eyes open." After a few minutes, discuss why this method of communicating to each other was the best. Write the factors involved on the board.
5. Have students form three equal lines. Tell them you are going to play the telephone game. Give the first person in line a message which he is expected to whisper to the next person and so on down the line. Ask the last person in line to say out loud what he heard. Do this with two or three messages and note discrepancies. Discuss with students, "What do you think happened?" (Students should conclude that one reason for the distortion was that some people left out words or changed words to give the message a different meaning.)

EVALUATION:
Note students' actions and verbal responses. Especially note nonverbal responses of students during the game.

Evaluation of the entire program in which Gestalt game approaches play a prominent part has produced some interesting results. Evaluation of this exploratory program took place in inner-city schools with primarily black students and suburban schools with primarily white students.

As black-white relations are a central theme in several of the lesson plans, it was found that the black-white composition of classes using the plans was an important variable with respect to (1) how the games were played, and (2) how the games were received by participants. For example, in Lesson Plan 9, "Feeling Black," instructions varied with the black-white variable. In an inner-city school the teacher said, "While standing in front of the mirror, imagine that your face is white." (All students in the class were black.) In a suburban school (all white) the teacher said, "While looking at yourself in the mirror, imagine that your face is black." In another classroom with black and white students, the teacher said, "Imagine that your face is just the opposite color." Adjustments in the original lesson plan were easily made by the classroom teacher.

Whether a teacher was black or white also proved to be an important variable to be considered. A black teacher in an all black school used pictures of blacks while teaching Lesson Plan 4, "Facts and Values." No objections were raised. When a white teacher in the same classroom situation used pictures of blacks, five black students related their objections to a black teacher in the school. They said in a matter-of-fact rather than hostile manner, "We already know about black people. Why doesn't he (the white teacher) show pictures of his own people?" There was also some feeling on the part of the five students that the teacher could not speak for black people but could speak for white people.

Whether the teacher was black or white, the emotional nature of the subject matter provided us with an interesting response to Lesson Plan 4, "Facts and Values." A white teacher in an all black class was drawing statements from the national scene in order to determine whether or not students understood the distinction between factual claims and opinions. Students indicated their understanding of the distinction by correctly answering four or five questions. The teacher then said, "How about the statement 'Black is beautiful?' Is that a factual claim or opinion?" The students responded in unison, "That's a fact." The teacher, somewhat shocked, responded, "I think white is beautiful. Is 'white is beautiful' a factual claim or opinion?" The students once again responded in unison, "That's an opinion." At this point the teacher paused for what seemed to be several minutes, approached the board and wrote, "I think black is beautiful. Therefore it's beautiful." He then said to the class, "Are you saying this because you think something is a fact it necessarily follows that it is a fact?" With this statement there was considerable class discussion after which the bell, signalling the end of the hour, rang.

Although we anticipated some objections from parents to the use of humanistic content and to the Gestalt games themselves, no objections have been registered with participating schools thus far. Most objections have come from fellow teachers largely for logistical or technical reasons rather than philosophical reasons. Colleagues have often reminded teachers using the games to "keep the noise down." One teacher voiced what must have been in the minds of several teachers in the same school: "How can children learn with all that noise and confusion?" By *confusion* she meant movement around the room. Some newer teachers who used the games initially found them to be a threat to their concept of an orderly classroom—order giving them security for they then felt they had control. These same teachers soon learned that the Gestalt games acted as a kind of "safety valve" in the school which let students work out many of their feelings—often feelings that were aggressive in nature.

A major finding as a result of evaluation of the program was that *teachers had to inform students that they did not have to play any of the games if they did not want to.* Forced participation of students resulted in ineffective games, but, more importantly, it violated humanism. Students who chose not to play usually made this decision on the basis of what they thought good learning was rather than in response to the controversial subject matter in the games. In a sixth-grade class two students pretended to be reading their texts while peeping at peers playing the games. These students felt that one learned by reading the text rather than by "playing games." The teacher in the classroom noted as an aside that this was the only time during the year that these two students ever read the text.

A critical question remains to be asked, a question that is the subject of further evaluation of the program: Will playing the Gestalt games affect the behavior of students in real-life situations outside the classroom? It is possible that the student will play out the action in class thinking that he has really accomplished something without ever crossing the threshold to social action. He may acquire humanistic knowledge and ways of behaving in the classroom without the games influencing his basic belief system.

In conclusion, we find the Gestalt game approach to be *one promising alternative* to traditional education in elementary schools. It is our belief that the Gestalt game approach with its emphasis on subject matter that deals with man's social successes and failures and on teaching and learning processes that focus on man's basic qualities is a powerful technique for beginning humanistic instruction.

Notes

1. Robert F. Mager, *Preparing Instructional Objectives* (Palo Alto, California: Fearon Publishers, 1962), p. 15.
2. Jerome S. Bruner, *The Process of Education* (New York: Vintage Books, 1960), p. 14.
3. J. C. R. Licklider, *Libraries of the Future* (Cambridge, Massachusetts: Massachusetts Institute of Technology Press, 1965), p. 15.
4. R. Murray Thomas, *Social Differences in the Classroom* (New York: David McKay Company, Inc., 1965), p. 157.
5. Fannie R. Shaftel, *Role-playing for Social Values* (Englewood Cliffs, New Jersey: Prentice-Hall, Inc., 1967), p. 10.

Case Study Approaches

CHAPTER 6

The case study strategy we have developed for elementary school instruction is based on the same value judgments or philosophical commitments as is the Gestalt game strategy described in the previous chapter. These commitments are spelled out in the introduction to this section of the book. Such value judgments are in fact the *objectives* for the use of case studies in our program. Unlike the previous strategy involving Gestalt games, suggested objectives are not a part of our case study strategy. Instead, we rely on the elementary school teacher to formulate his own day-to-day objectives as he uses case studies in a variety of situations.

The case study *method*, often used in professional schools such as law and medicine, is relatively new to both elementary and secondary schools, but particularly elementary schools. There are two main ways in which the case study method is used with respect to humanistic instruction: (1) to illustrate conclusions of the teacher, students, or others; and (2) to stimulate thought on what the teacher, students, or others consider to be controversial subjects.

Materials used in implementing the case study strategy are simply the cases themselves. Cases may be taken from the mass media or a variety of other sources including the first-hand experiences of learners —teachers and students.

We have found that one of the best ways to *evaluate* what happens when cases are used is through the use of audio and video tapes. Rather than treating evaluation as a separate section at the end of this chapter, we have chosen to include excerpts from tape recordings in the main body of this chapter.

In working with elementary school teachers in developing cases for classroom use, we have identified four fairly broad topical areas that serve as humanistic subject matter for cases: (1) student school and community life; (2) student health; (3) aesthetics; and (4) substantive issues. These four areas are considered humanistic because, as with the Ges-

115

talt games, they stress man's achievements and failures, and also, because they stress man's natural qualities of independence, self-reliance, thinking, valuing, and feeling. In the following section of this chapter we will discuss briefly each topical area after which we will include examples of cases developed at various grade levels and a description of what happened when used in elementary school classes.

Student School and Community Life

Many rules exist which directly influence students' behavior in the classroom, the school, and the larger community in which they live. Rules for behavior are not necessarily written but may instead be achieved (formulated and enforced) through other kinds of verbal and nonverbal communication. The rule may be as simple as "Raise your hand before speaking" or as complex as "Adjust to the teacher's mood on a given day."

Classroom Life

It is natural given the number of hours a teacher and students spend in the classroom that this environment is the subject of many rules. Behavior that conforms to such rules is reinforced whereas deviant behavior is the target for modification. The greater the emotion felt by the teacher with respect to enforcing a particular rule at a particular time, the greater the press on the student to conform. On such occasions, teaching becomes highly prescriptive and *analysis* of such behavior becomes less important than *consensus* as to the validity of the rule. The case approach can give teachers and students distance from an event so that analysis can take place. At the same time empathy with those involved in a case can be achieved.

The following case was used by a kindergarten teacher to reinforce appropriate classroom behavior. She used an example of inappropriate classroom behavior from her afternoon class as a case for her morning students to examine.

> In our afternoon kindergarten, most of the children are good helpers. They come in quietly, try not to bother others, listen carefully, and follow directions. A few days ago, a boy ran into the room, shouted while he was taking off his wraps, disturbed others, and in general upset our class.

The teacher began a discussion by asking, "Why do you think the boy behaved that way?" Some of the students' responses were:

Bill: He probably has too much energy.

Jill: Maybe he isn't old enough for school.

Jim: Maybe he doesn't know the rules.

Sue: Maybe he acts this way because he isn't used to this school. Was he new?

The discussion then moved to this question, "How do you think the other children in the class felt?" Several of the students' responses were:

Bob: They probably thought he was bad.

Jim: They thought he shouldn't come to school if he was going to be naughty.

Jane: They were probably mad.

Another question asked by the teacher was, "What do you think should have been done about this boy?"

Jill: Send him to the principal.

Tim: Have him sit in a corner.

John: Kick him out of school if he is too bad.

Jim: Have a talk with him.

Finally, the teacher asked, "How could we help this boy?"

Bob: Show him how to behave.

Sue: Teach him the rules.

Bill: Everybody try to be his friend.

By using a case example from her other class, the teacher achieved a certain detachment that allowed her to find out some things about her students and herself. "Some of the students mirrored me," she commented. "not only in the terms they used but in their physical expressions and tone of voice." She continued, "I really began to think about some of the things I say and do and what effect they have on my children. I also found out something about how their parents apparently treat them when they misbehave."

School Life Outside of Class

Elementary school children are expected to be kind, considerate, and trustworthy on the way to and from school, on the playground, in the halls, the lavatories, and the cafeteria. Lunchroom behavior is the subject of the following case. The case was used in a second-grade class where most of the students eat their lunch at school.

> George attends the 72nd Street School. He is ten years old and is in the fourth grade. He stays for hot lunch every day because both of his parents are working.
>
> George's behavior is generally poor both in school and on the playground. He is constantly the center of trouble in the hallways and in the lunchroom. Because of his disruptive behavior in the lunchroom, he has been told that if he continues to misbehave drastic measures will be taken by the principal.
>
> One day last week a small child dropped a tray of food as he was walking toward a table. While the teacher on lunchroom duty and an assistant were helping the child and diverting the other children, George began throwing grapes at the other end of the room. Suddenly several other boys joined in and grapes were flying everywhere.

After reading the case, the teacher held a discussion with her second graders. She asked them what they felt the principal should do with George. Students responded as follows:

Bill: Send him home.

Jane: Expel George for a couple of days.

Jim: No hot lunch for George for a week.

John: Sit him in the corner for the rest of the day.

Larry: Slam his head against the wall.

Sue: He deserves to be scolded and punished.

Bob: Make him write a thousand times, "I must be good in the lunchroom or I will have to write some more."

Ann: His mother and dad should come to school.

Jack: Big kids act terrible in the lunchroom.

Jim: Some kids in our room act awful.

From here the discussion moved into why it is necessary to behave in the cafeteria and how students can help each other to maintain an orderly but pleasant atmosphere in the cafeteria. The teacher had achieved her objective. Namely, students should behave in certain ways in the lunchroom for certain reasons.

The following case was used in a fifth-grade class. Students were asked to read the case and then write a few sentences in response to the question, "If you were the principal, what would you do?"

Sam would do anything to keep blame from being placed on him. He would even lie—and did very often. Pretty soon, no one would trust Sam's word. They couldn't be sure he wasn't telling another lie.

One day, Sam and three other friends—Joe, George, and Clem—were in the boys' lavatory during a break.

"Let's see how many paper towels we can put up on the light fixtures!" said Joe. George started right in but Clem and Sam thought they shouldn't do it. They just watched.

After a few minutes of fun and noise-making, a teacher walked into the lavatory to see what the commotion was all about. Noticing the paper towels on the fixture, the teacher said, "Okay, now, who did this?"

All of the boys blamed each other. They were sent to the office to see the principal. Sam had been there several times and the principal knew his reputation.

Sam, when questioned, claimed he had just been watching. Clem supported what Sam said but Joe and George blamed everything on Sam.

Students responded as follows:

- Loreen: If I were the principal I would tell them to tell the truth or not give them any lavatory breaks for a month. I would give them all the same punishment because Clem and Sam stood there watching but they didn't stop them or go tell the teacher. I think they were just as guilty as the other boys.
- Bill: I would punish all the boys, because none of them would say they did it. Their punishment would be to write a theme and stay after school. Sam probably felt bad and angry and wanted to strike back at the two guilty boys.
- Mike: I would ask the teacher where they were standing when he came in and judge by that.
- Sharon: If Sam was always the liar, why would Clem support his answer. I would think Sam is telling the truth and so I would punish Joe and George.
- Jim: I'd keep on questioning them until a different story came out. I'd question Sam the most because of his bad reputation. If the truth didn't come out, I'd call their mother and father.
- David: I would probably question them more and then call their parents to punish all of them. Maybe the two boys would

> say they did it then. If they didn't tell I would make them clean up the lavatory and have no lavatory breaks unless a teacher was there. I would have them stay after school every night until someone told me that they did it.
>
> Jack: I would punish all the boys because they were all in the lavatory laughing and making noise. The punishment would be no lavatory breaks for two weeks and a note sent home to be signed by the parents and brought back.
>
> Randy: I'd talk to Sam and Clem alone and see what they said. Then I'd combine their stories and see what I came up with. I think Clem was a nice boy and wouldn't tell a lie so I'd believe Sam and punish Joe and George.

The written responses were then discussed in relation to causes of the events, effects of the event, and the possible courses of action.

The teacher reacted in the following manner to the discussion of the case: "Students were really involved and liked dealing with an issue as relevant as this one. The next time I might end the case when the teacher walks into the lavatory so that the children could provide an ending at this point. Or I might include the principal's decision on the case and let my students react to that. By having each student write his response to the case prior to the discussion I found out what all of them thought rather than just a few who would normally talk in class."

Community Life

Safety is a major subject in the elementary school curriculum. The teacher not only wants to support safe practices in the school but also in the child's neighborhood or community. The following case was used in a first-grade classroom.

> One afternoon in spring, some children were playing ball in the street. When cars came along, the children would move to the sides of the street. But when one car drove up, several children didn't see him and stayed in the street until the driver had to slow down and honk his horn. The children started to yell at the driver for spoiling their game. Then the driver got out of his car and started to walk over to them. What do you think should happen next?

The children listened attentively because of similar experiences. There are few sidewalks in the neighborhood so that they frequently play in the street. They commented as follows:

> Sue: The driver should call the police because the kids wouldn't get out of the road.

CASE STUDY APPROACHES 121

Bill: The driver should tell the principal to announce on the speaker that kids should stay out of the road.

Bob: The driver should get the principal over there and should talk to the kids' mothers. The kids should have to stay in for two weeks.

Irene: The parents should hit the kids.

Jack: The driver should yell, "Get out of the road. It's an emergency. My mother's having a baby."

Sue: No, that's a lie. The man should call the police.

As the discussion progressed the teacher asked the students *why* the event they described should happen and how they would feel if it happened to them.

The following is a case study used in a kindergarten class:

Timmy is a five year old boy in a kindergarten class. He is very tall and people often think he is much older than five. At Christmas time he received some ice skates. He used them almost every day and soon became a good skater. At first, Timmy's mother went with him to his school's ice rink, but lately he and his friends have gone there alone.

One day Timmy's friends were busy after school and so Timmy went to the ice rink alone. When he got to his school he found the shelter was closed and a sign was on the entrance to the rink. He didn't know what the sign said but he decided to put his skates on by the side of the rink. He skated for quite some time even though it wasn't much fun to skate alone.

Suddenly he heard someone calling his name and he turned around to see the man who cares for the rink. Timmy waved and kept on skating doing all of the fancy tricks he had learned. Then he heard the man call again, "Get off the ice. Can't you read the sign?" Timmy knew the man wanted him to get off the ice—and fast.

He skated over to the side of the rink and started to ask why he should get off the ice. The man didn't stop scolding long enough for Timmy to ask. The man was very angry and said, "A big boy like you should know how to read by now. Don't you ever come to this rink again or I'll kick you off for good."

At this point students were asked to put themselves in Timmy's place and tell how they would feel if they were he. The following responses were given:

Eileen: It isn't Timmy's fault. If he is only five and in kindergarten he doesn't know how to read yet.

James: I would feel sad because the man hollered at me and I didn't know how to read the sign yet.

Susan: I would be afraid because the man might hurt me.

Bill: Timmy should ask someone what the sign said.

Jim: I would be angry because he told me to get off. It isn't my fault.

Janet: I would run home.

Larry: I would too.

Ann: I'd tell the man I was sorry.

Bob: The man was so angry because the ice might be soft and if Timmy broke it other kids wouldn't be able to skate.

Sheryl: Timmy wouldn't be afraid if the man would talk softly.

John: I would feel bad, but I think the rule is a dumb rule. If the ice was good why couldn't he skate?

Bette: I think the rule should be changed.

As the discussion continued it became evident that the students realized that the man did not recognize Timmy's inability to read signs, but still felt that he was rude in not listening to Timmy's explanation. A few began to question the wisdom of the rule itself.

In reacting to the following case another rule and its enforcement were discussed.

Last Saturday two boys were caught by the police in the city's bus parking lot. The boys were 12 and 13 years old. They told the police that they were only playing and didn't do any harm to the busses. They said there wasn't room in their neighborhood to play. There were signs saying DANGER—KEEP OUT. The police took the boys to the police station and called their parents to pick them up. They were not arrested.

The teacher focused the discussion on three questions: Was the rule a wise one? Were the police fair in their actions? And, if you were the boys, how would you feel toward the police? Some of the comments the fifth-grade students wrote were:

Jack: The rule was stupid especially since the boys didn't have any place else to play. I think they should let the boys go because they did not do one thing wrong. But if I were one of the boys I would not like it and I would not like to have the policeman call my mother or father and tell that I was down by the police station. I did not do anything wrong.

Bob: I think the boys were wrong and the police did the right thing in calling their parents. I'd thank the police because they taught me something and I'd be scared also.

Sue: The police were fair for the boys were old enough to read the sign. If I were the boys I would be asking for it by trespassing.

John: The boys were wrong but the cops shouldn't arrest them, just warn them. If I was the boy I would be scared because my ma and dad would have killed me!

Jim: The boys were right to be there for they didn't hurt anybody and anyway there aren't many good places to play around here.

Don: I'd feel mad that I was caught but what the police did was rite. At nite it would have been worse.

The class discussion that followed the written comments was similar to answers students gave in their writing. The case had served its function: it opened the floor for a discussion of different points of view on a controversial subject.

Conclusion

In reviewing the cases used for the students' school and community life, we can see that the teachers involved used such cases to examine rules and behavior. Analysis discussion dealt with reasons for deviant behavior, what, if any, reprimand should be given, and reasons for the rule.

Student Health

Elementary school teachers have traditionally been interested in the physical well-being of their charges. Students are expected to dress warmly when going out in cold weather, eat the proper foods, get plenty of sleep, and have certain attitudes toward the use of tobacco, alcohol, and drugs. School systems are frequently highly prescriptive in the area of student health. Such prescriptions, especially with respect to tobacco, alcohol, and drugs, are often a part of the state legal code. In California, for example, principals annually sign an affidavit swearing (1) that certain subjects are included in the curriculum and (2) that these subjects are treated in the proper manner. For example, state law requires that the harmful effects of tobacco, alcohol, and drugs be taught in the curriculum.

A second-grade teacher noted that some of her students became sleepy and lethargic as the morning progressed. She discovered that they had had little or no breakfast. As the school had no breakfast program, she decided to use a case in order to encourage the students to eat breakfast at home. The following case was used:

> I was talking with another teacher on the playground and she said that some of her students didn't eat any breakfast. What do you think happens if you don't eat any breakfast?

The second graders replied:

Tammy: You get hungry.

Jill: And sleepy.

Tom: It's hard to run at recess time. (Tom was identified as one student who failed to eat breakfast.)

Jim: Your stomach feels real light and funny.

The teacher and students then discussed what constituted a good breakfast, and why breakfast is essential for most people.

The following case focusing on a marijuana pusher is more controversial than breakfast:

> Al is 17 years old and 5′ 9″ tall. He is in the 11th grade. He has long hair, wears a leather fringed jacket, faded jeans, and usually wears flashy clothes.
>
> Al is frequently in trouble in school. He is loud, boisterous, and the leader of a group not part of the mainstream of the school.
>
> Al drives a vintage Chevie and was picked up recently for speeding. His driver's license was suspended for 60 days. Recently he was referred to the juvenile home after he was picked up at a school dance for being drunk and disorderly. The subsequent police investigation disclosed that Al was pushing marijuana in school. School officials were informed of this and a police check was made of his locker. One marijuana cigarette (joint) was found along with a coke bottle filled with gin.
>
> When confronted with evidence, Al denied the items were his. He said that ten other students knew his locker combination and frequently used it for storage. Al felt pressured, became angry, and started exchanging insults with the police officers and school officials. A scuffle resulted and Al was taken to the detention home loudly shouting his innocence.

Sixth-grade students reacted as follows when asked to write a few sentences about the case:

Lee: Al's past made no difference for he could be telling the truth in this case. Al might have done some stupid and wrong things but this is know reason right away to judge that he's wrong. If he did push marijuana it's no worse than selling booze. In fact it's not as bad.

James: I think a kid like that should be locked up because I know a kid the same way and he is wrecking his life and the lives of many other people.

Syl: The cops were rotten the way they moved in on Al. School officials shouldn't be able to go through your personal things whenever they want to. Al wasn't pushing anything hard and so what's the big deal.

Dick: If he wants drugs thats up to him and its also up to him not to get caught. When they did catch him if he would of behaved better he probably would of gotten off better. Usually its the trouble makers that have drugs and the ones that dress extremely different. If he had drugs and didn't want anyone to know he should of acted different and no one would of suspected it. Why make a big deal about pot anyway?

The case acted as an introduction to the study of drugs with special attention given to motivation for using drugs and effects of drug use. The new teacher, visibly affected by student attitudes toward marijuana, made this unit of study far more open-ended than she originally intended.

Aesthetics

Value judgments as to what is beautiful are the subject matter of aesthetics. Aesthetics may well be the most overlooked area of the elementary school curriculum. And yet, teachers and students make value judgments as to what is beautiful throughout the curriculum in general and particularly in the humanities part of the curriculum. Think for a moment of your own biases as to what constitutes "good" art, music, and writing, and then ask if you reveal such biases to your students. For example, one teacher asked her students to bring phonograph records to be played during the last period of the day. When one student brought in a record by the Monkees, the teacher said, "Now, we don't play records like that in school, do we!!!" The teacher's degrading comment was obviously nonhumanistic.

The following case was used during a three-week unit for fifth graders on the topic, "What is an American?" The teacher had students react to excerpts from the writings of foreign visitors to the United States

—people such as Winston Churchill, Frances Trollope, Lord Bryce, and Alexis de Tocqueville. The teacher centered the class' attention on authors' writing styles as well as content. The following case is an excerpt from *The American Character,* by the bright and witty Scotsman, D. W. Brogan.

> The schools, the movies—above all, advertising—taught the Americans that they led the world in everything that really mattered. Not one American in a thousand, for instance, reflected that the most important modern invention, the internal-combustion engine, had been invented in Germany and perfected in France, that the American contribution was belated and secondary. There was nothing strange in the Russians being able to make the atom bomb; it was certain that sooner or later they would do so.[1]

Although the teacher had more specific questions in mind concerning content and writing style, he initially asked his students, "What do you think of what I just read?"

Bill: Who cares about the combustion-engine anyway? I've never seen one.

Larry: How do you think your dad's car runs! That's a combustion engine!

Bill: Yeh! I guess so.

Teacher: Let me read the paragraph again and you tell me how it sounds to you. Remember our discussion about authors' writing styles. What do you think of this author's writing style? (Read passage again.)

Susan: I like it! It's really smooth. It sounds like he's right here talking to us.

Dick: I think it's too smooth. It's like some songs where you like the music but never hear the words.

Teacher: What's wrong with being too smooth?

Dick: He could say anything and you would agree.

Teacher: How do the rest of you feel about the author's writing style?

June: I like it because it isn't boring. It's kind of funny too.

Teacher: I'm interested in why you find it funny.

June: Well, it's true that we think we're the best in everything. Movies and advertising do tell us that.

Leroy: He does what you do sometimes when you teach. You blast something in a nice way. It *is* smooth.

Students were then asked to write a paragraph in which they discussed why they liked or disliked the author's style. In the latter, they were asked to rewrite the excerpt in their own way conveying the same ideas as the author.

Substantive Issues

Controversial issues of a more substantial nature elicit a high degree of emotional involvement. Race relations, environmental pollution, overpopulation, and wars serve as examples of substantive issues as do many of the problems and accomplishments listed in Table V. We feel that case studies should primarily focus on substantive issues.

In our discussion of substantive issues we will include (1) cases used in selected elementary school classrooms, (2) a transcript of students' and teacher's discussion comments, and (3) annotations in which we describe operations in which the students were engaged as they reacted to the issue at hand.

The following case was used in a fourth-grade class in the inner city. Fifteen of the twenty-five students were black, five Mexican-American or Puerto Rican, and five white. The school has low middle-class families in it and the neighborhood is considered to be run-down.

Case Study Number One[*]

"You owe another dime, my friend," uttered the bus driver, dryly.

"Who, me?" inquired Melvin, a sixteen-year-old black youth.

"That's right. It costs a quarter to ride this bus, not fifteen cents. Come on an' give the company another ten cents, O.K.?"

"What do you mean? I put a quarter in already. Somebody else must have put in fifteen cents. Not me."

"Look," stated the bus driver obviously growing impatient, "there were four passengers getting on the bus. You were the last one. You put fifteen cents in the box. What's it going to be, huh? Are you going to pay up, or what?"

"I told you that I didn't put no fifteen cents in there," replied Melvin. Now growing defiant, he concluded, "I ain't putting no more money in!"

After about five seconds of silent staring, the bus driver closed the doors to the bus, and swung away from the corner and into the down-

---

[*] This case study was developed in a Civic Education project under the leadership of Dale Flowers, University of California, Santa Cruz. Dale Brubaker participated in the project.

town traffic. Melvin walked back in the bus and sat at an empty seat some three rows back. All appeared settled, although Melvin was still somewhat angry at the confrontation which had occurred in front of some fifteen passengers, all white.

Presently the bus stopped in front of an all-night hamburger eatery. The driver got off of the bus as if to purchase coffee. About five minutes later, the driver returned, without coffee, and again moved the bus into the downtown traffic.

At the next stop, the driver deposited three passengers out of the back door, and gained five through the front door. One of the new passengers was an acquaintance of Melvin's and upon recognition, moved to the back of the bus and sat next to him.

The bus remained at the stop, idling noisely. No passengers boarded the bus. The driver casually sat in his seat looking out the large front window.

A patrol car cruised up next to the bus and parked somewhat cater-corner in front of it. Two young police officers got out of the car, hitched their pants, and walked to the front door of the bus. The driver stood up from his seat and met the officers as they boarded.

One officer pulled a small white tablet from his pocket and began to write in it. The bus driver, obviously angry, talked rapidly and suddenly pointed toward the back of the bus where Melvin was sitting with his friend. Without looking up, the young officer nodded his head and continued to write. The second officer, standing somewhat to the rear of the driver, and his partner began to visually scan the passengers seated on the bus. He said something to his partner who again nodded his head without looking up, continuing to write in his tablet.

The driver led the two officers to the back of the bus and stopped next to the seat accommodating Melvin and his friend. Pointing at Melvin he stated: "He just walked on the bus and put fifteen cents in the box. When I caught him doing it, he tried to get smart saying "I ain't putting no more money in."

"Yeah, O.K." said the first officer. "Let us handle it." Then, tablet and pencil in hand, he looked at Melvin and asked, "Is that true young man? Is what the driver said true?"

"No, it isn't," replied Melvin. "I had twenty five cents in my pocket —just enough to ride the bus home—I put it in the box. I don't have any more money on me; that's how I know I put a quarter in the box."

"I see," replied the officer. "Was this young man sitting next to you here with you at the time?"

"No he just got on the bus," replied Melvin.

"Oh."

"I want him off my bus" yelled the driver. "Get him off of here. These wise kids always giving drivers trouble. It's gotten so none of the drivers want to drive through the East Oakland area."

"Yeah, O.K." said the officer. "Will you please let us handle this, huh?"

"All I know is that this bus is not going to move 'till you get that wise guy off here. What do we pay you guys for anyway. Bus drivers are assaulted all over the East Bay, and I can't even get two officers to help me out when I point out the criminal."

"But," intoned the second officer, "It's your word against this kid here. You said he didn't pay; he says he did."

"There you go taking the side of the colored. It seems like today colored can get away with anything. They rob, beat, and shoot us bus operators all over Oakland; now all you can do is take their side."

"Look, sir, nobody's taking sides here."

"Well, get this trouble-maker off my bus."

"Just on your word, you want us to ignore what he has to say in his own defense?" asked the second officer.

"Look," hollered the bus driver, "I been driving buses in the East Bay for the past five years. For fifteen years before that I drove buses in Chicago and Detroit. I know wise-guy trouble-makers when I see them. Now I'm not saying all colored people are bad, but you know yourself they commit more crimes than other people. Now here we find a colored boy who is so bold that he just walks on a bus and says that he ain't going to pay his fare.

"Don't call me boy and I ain't colored" says Melvin, balefully staring at the driver. "I'm a man and I'm black. I'm a black man."

"See?" shouts the driver. "I told you he was a trouble-maker. He's talking about Black Power and all that stuff. Ever since that Carmichael character, these people been expecting something for nothing."

"Now wait a minute," interrupted the first officer. "Let's not get off into a discussion of race relations."

"What's your badge number?" asks the driver. "If you don't get this guy off this bus, I'm going to report you to your department. As it is, you've made me late on my route."

"I'm not getting off this bus" exclaimed Melvin. "I paid my fare, and I'm not getting off."

"What about making an exception this one time?" the second officer asked the driver. "Do you think that the company could stand to lose a dime?"

"That's right," sighed the driver, "coddling criminals. I've always suspected that you people handled criminals with kid gloves."

"Well, will you let him ride this time?"

"Hell no I won't!"

"Well, I'm not paying no more money, and I'm not going to get off this bus 'till it drops me off in the front of my house."

"Get off the bus!" encouraged a few passengers on the bus. "Get the hell off the bus; we want to get home."

"That's right!" exclaimed the driver. "You see, the passengers are on my side. They know this guy slipped on the bus."

"The two officers looked at each other. The first sighed and shrugged his shoulder. The second did the same. "Come on," they said to Melvin. "You have to leave the bus."

In analyzing the use of the case in this particular fourth-grade inner-city classroom, we have included classroom comments—written and verbal—and annotations interpreting the comments.

Initially, the teacher had the students read the case and write any feelings they had about the incident. She did this so all the students would take a stand and commit themselves in a form—writing—that they could refer to throughout the analysis of the case.

	Classroom Comments	*Annotations*
Wendell:	"I don't think it's fair. If he was white the bus driver won't have done that. I don't think the bus driver was fair."	
Shar:	"I don't think it fair and he should of got his money back. Maybe he did pay the right amount."	
Diana:	"I would tell the bus driver that he did put in all the money he was suppose to. Or I would give the black man 10 cents."	
George:	"I think that the bus driver was not fair. The cop was not fair either because he didn't ask the black man as much as the driver."	Common reaction for students linked police and driver together as part of "white establishment." (A common response in suburban schools is to pit older generation—driver and police—against youth—Melvin.)
Bob:	"If he was white it wouldn't of happened. Just because the man was black the bus driver said he did not have enough money. The driver was prejudiced. The policeman was fair because he was doing his duty."	No role conflict in student's mind as far as police were concerned; role conflict for bus driver—he didn't behave as student felt he should have, given his job.

At this point in the use of the case, the teacher felt that two objectives were important: (1) the clarification of terms not understood by all of the students; and (2) agreement by students as to what facts

CASE STUDY APPROACHES   131

could be drawn from the case and what factual questions needed to be asked. Therefore, her first question was, "Bob said the bus driver was prejudiced. What does the *prejudiced* mean?"

	Classroom Comments	Annotations
Shar:	"It means you don't like somebody because he's black."	The definition of terms is an important aspect of the analysis of controversial issues according to Oliver and Shaver.[2]
Bob:	"Not just black. You can be prejudiced against people for different reasons."	Student responses, mainly nonverbal, indicated to the teacher that students understood the term *prejudiced*.

After several definitions, a student attempted a summary, "Some people are prejudiced or don't like other people because they're black, brown, red, short, fat or whatever. In other words, even though they don't know the other person they don't like him because he has one of these things about him."

	Classroom Comments	Annotations
Teacher:	"What *facts*—what we know for sure—can you tell about the situation Melvin was in?"	
Janet:	"Melvin was kicked off the bus and didn't have a ride."	
George:	"The driver was prejudiced."	
Teacher:	"How do you know that?"	Students reviewed driver's comments and especially his use of words such as "colored boy." Class agreed that driver was prejudiced.
		Students continued to identify facts and teacher included these facts in her summary of case.
Teacher:	"What do we still need to know about the situation? What questions should we ask and try to answer to help us understand what happened?"	
Bob:	"We still don't know for sure if Melvin put in fifteen cents or a quarter."	

	Classroom Comments	Annotations
Teacher:	"We read that the police were young, but what were they—black, white, brown?"	The teacher hoped that some student would ask about the race of the policemen involved. Nobody did and therefore she raised the question.

Students hesitated for a minute and then quickly looked at the case again. |
Bob:	"It doesn't say. I guess that we all thought they were white."	
Teacher:	"Why?"	
George:	"Most cops are white."	
Teacher:	"Then we do need to know if the police were black, brown, or white."	Student responses at this point indicated that the race of policemen was an important matter for the most part. A few students didn't think this was important for police are police no matter what. That is, their role is defined regardless of race.

The class then proceeded to the important matter of what values were involved in the case, how some of these values were in conflict, and alternative resolutions for such conflicts.

	Classroom Comments	Annotations
Teacher:	"Let's talk about what different people in the bus thought about what happened. We'll talk about what they really thought was important—and we'll call this their *values*."

"What did the people riding in the bus want?" | |
George:	"They were mad. They wanted to get where they were goin' and the fight slowed 'em down."	Teacher wrote *efficiency* on board and class noted its meaning. Efficiency the general value drawn from concrete situation.
Teacher:	"What did the police want or value do you feel?"	
Warren:	"Blood!"	

CASE STUDY APPROACHES

	Classroom Comments	Annotations
Teacher:	"What do you mean?"	
Warren:	"They wanted to clean up the mess—the whole mess."	
Teacher:	"Say a little more about what you mean, Warren."	Teacher wrote *keep the peace* and *order* on the board. Students indicated understanding of terms. General value drawn from concrete situation. No conflict between general values felt by students as yet.
Warren:	"They thought the bus driver was stupid and the kids were wrong to be noisy and angry. They just wanted to stop the fight—clean up the whole mess without taking sides."	
Teacher:	"By looking at your heads shaking it looks like you agree. The police wanted to stop the fighting, return to normal, and yet not take sides."	
	"What did the bus driver want?"	
James:	"He wanted to show he was the man—the boss tellin' everybody what to do."	Teacher wrote *authority* on board.
Bob:	"He had a problem all right. Kept talking about all his experience and things."	Teacher wrote *experience* on board.
Teacher:	"Are you saying that he didn't want anything to change and he was the boss in the bus."	Teacher wrote *tradition* on board. Class indicated understanding.
Class:	"Yes."	
Teacher:	"What did Melvin want or value?"	
Richard:	"He just wanted to do his thing—to be left alone. He was tired of bein' put down—just like all blacks."	
Bob:	"Yeh, but if he didn't put the quarter in he was just hustlin' the driver."	

	Classroom Comments	*Annotations*
James:	"He put the money in!"	
Teacher:	"Remember, we said that one thing we didn't know for sure was if Melvin put the money in or not."	
	"Let's just say that we do know that Melvin didn't like what happened whether or not he put in the money."	Teacher wrote *anti-authority* on board. Students indicated understanding of *authority* and *anti* or against *authority*. Conflict of values now evident.
	"What did Melvin's friend want or value?"	
Shar:	"He sticked up for his friend just as he should of."	Teacher wrote *loyalty to friend* on board.
Teacher:	"Let's talk about what you think should have happened. How would you have changed the way things happened?"	
James:	"They should have kicked the bus driver off the bus."	Teacher and class discuss alternative solutions to conflict situation.
Wendell:	"Yeh, fired him."	
Teacher:	"How could that have happened?"	
Wendell:	"Tell the driver's boss."	
James:	"Nobody listens to kids."	
Bob:	"You could have your parents tell the driver's boss."	
Teacher:	"What else could have happened?"	
Richard:	"The cops could have put in a dime for Melvin."	
James:	"Yeh, or somebody in the bus should of."	
Bob:	"The police should have given Melvin a ride instead of just leaving him there."	
Diana:	"Yeh!"	

Conclusion

The main value of case studies lies in their ability to stimulate thought about humanistic content. When student reactions to cases are recorded, usually on tape or in writing, they provide the teacher and students with tangible evidence that can be reviewed and discussed.

Case studies should also help students identify their own attitudes and values after which such values can be subjected to analysis and reconstruction. Students should also be motivated to acquire additional information as a result of the use of case studies. Finally, case study approaches can aid the student by having him empathize with various parties in a conflict situation.

Case studies based on humanistic content are relatively easy to develop. Teachers can create them from actual events that they or their students experience or from the experiences of others which one hears or reads about.

Notes

1. D. W. Brogan, *The American Character* (New York: Vintage Books, 1956), p. 208.
2. Donald W. Oliver, and James P. Shaver, *Teaching Public Issues in High School* (Boston: Houghton-Mifflin Company, 1966).

Studying Emerging Problems

CHAPTER 7

To be committed to humanistic instruction in the classroom is not sufficient to insure that humanism will actually be developed and maintained in the classroom. For this event to occur, as we have seen, specific humanistic behaviors of teachers and students and humanistic substance or content need to be identified and used. Humanistic process and substance can be initiated in a variety of ways. We feel that two of the most significant are Gestalt games and case studies. These approaches or strategies are effective "starters" of humanistic activity. They serve teachers by providing them with a vehicle that immediately introduces humanistic content and naturally results in many humanistic teacher and student behaviors. Games and case studies, however, cannot be and are not intended to be employed continuously in classrooms. Nevertheless, if students are to become humanistic persons, humanistic instruction must pervade the classroom; it must occupy a large segment of the total classroom day, if not the total day itself. This extension of humanistic instruction from the Gestalt games and case studies can occur by developing the ideas, interests, and problems that emerge from them. It can occur by using the games and cases as departure points for what Clements and his colleagues call study.[1] The games and cases themselves involve humanistic teaching and learning, but they can also generate more encompassing humanistic activity by stimulating study.

Study, according to Clements and his colleagues, can be summarized as being "inquiry that confronts the residue of social events."[2] Study involves three elements: thought, observation, and things. Thought refers primarily to questioning and the formulation of hypotheses. Observation refers to data collection, to finding evidence that exists, or, through instruments or tools, generating evidence. Things refer to the objects which one can observe and about which one can think. A thing can be a chapter in a book, a person, a photograph, or a broken piece of glass.

Two types of problems which students can study are knowledge problems and decision-action problems. Knowledge problems are problems. of understanding. Their solution brings deeper comprehension of an event or activity. Decision-action problems are problems of choice. Their solution brings guidelines for practice, and, hopefully, practice or action itself. The following examples may help clarify the difference between these two types of problems:

1. Knowledge problems
   a. Why is the bus company going out of business?
   b. Why are our urban centers losing population?
   c. Why did the Chicago stockyards close down?
2. Decision-action problems
   a. How can we help fight pollution?
   b. What can we do to stop the freeway from being built through the park?
   c. What should be done about the window breakage in our school?

From a humanistic standpoint both of these types of problems ought to be dealt with by elementary school students. In the remainder of this chapter a model of study is presented and an example of its use in dealing with a knowledge problem that emerged from a Gestalt game is described. In the next chapter decision-action problems and activities are discussed.

The model for study that Clements and his colleagues present is a general model that is derived from social science research methodology. The model consists of six elements:

1. Acquaintanceship

   The first step in study is acquaintanceship with the area or topic in which one may find a problem to study or investigate. Questions with research potential will not arise unless one is familiar with the particular area of concern. This acquaintanceship can result from some out-of-school activity or event such as a student's summer vacation in Los Angeles or a recent fight he had with his sister. Or, it can result from some in-school activity, such as a Gestalt game or case study analysis. From these two classroom activities a great deal of knowledge, insight, and feeling can be derived that may result in powerful questions for study.

2. The big question

   As a result of acquaintanceship, specific interests or doubts of students will hopefully emerge that will serve as humanistic questions for investigation. The big question stimulates study. It intrigues the student or students who posed it to the point where postponement of collecting data is painful. Worthwhile big questions are questions that not only intrigue students but also have developmental possibilities, are not directly answerable through typical classroom resources such as textbooks, and are appropriate for the ability level of the students for whom they are intended. Examples of questions that may serve as big questions are those presented in relation to teacher humanistic responding in Chapter 2.

The actual big question may be initiated by an individual student or group of students, or it may be the result of developing reacting teacher behavior and subsequent student responding. Also, the teacher may pose the big question in relation to a student's ideas or feelings.

3. Subquestions

    The big question is often not directly answerable. It needs to be translated into a series of subquestions which are directly answerable. These subquestions not only give direction to the collection of data but they define and clarify the big question. They should be formulated in a way that encourages observation and firsthand experiences.

    Subquestions will undoubtedly be an outgrowth of intense teacher-student interaction with teachers using developing reacting and various types of responding, and students asking questions, relating, responding, and also using developing reacting.

4. Data collection

    Following the formulation of subquestions, data collection can begin through the observation of things. Although some material can be acquired from second and thirdhand sources, if students are to become independent in their thoughts and values, they need to confront firsthand data in an effort to solve or compose answers to their subquestions.

    The teacher's role in data collection is to respond in a direct manner to students' questions concerning data and to suggest through relating or developing reacting data sources that may be fruitful for students.

5. Clarifying and organizing ideas

    As data begin to accumulate in relation to the subquestions, concepts need to be selected or hypotheses made that help to order and explain the data. Fundamental ideas from various disciplines such as role, institution, and interdependence are often useful. These notions may result in further subquestions and data collection.

Teacher developing reacting can be very effective in helping students to identify and apply clarifying concepts, as can direct and indirect responding at the appropriate times.

6. A report

Inquiry always ends in a report, an account of what was investigated and what was found. Constructing a concluding report helps the student criticize and synthesize his inquiry and it serves as a record of his investigations for others to examine. The report may not always contain a final answer or solution to a problem; it may contain a logical argument in support of a tentative answer.

Many exciting problems or big questions will emerge from Gestalt games and case studies that are suitable for study and that will extend humanistic process and content in the classroom. An example of study that resulted from a Gestalt game is the following inquiry into freeways. It resulted from role playing and subsequent discussion involved in the Landlord and Tenant Gestalt game that falls under the theme of Intergroup Relations. This particular problem could also have been a result of the Traffic game or the Use of Leisure game under the theme of Technological Change or the Back to Nature game under the theme of Urbanization..

The topic of freeways came up in the playing of the Landlord-Tenant game with a group of fifth graders when the student playing the landlord game gave property condemnation for freeway construction as a reason for asking the tenant to leave. In the follow-up discussion many students became interested in freeways and wanted to know if it was wise to destroy houses to make way for freeways. Through the teacher's skillful developing reacting a big question in which the total class was interested emerged. Their big question was: "Are freeways worth it?" (It should be noted that inquiry into a specific problem may not involve the entire class. A particular problem may be investigated by one student or perhaps a group of two or three students.)

Following identification of the big question one of the first decisions the class made was that they needed more general information about freeways. To become better acquainted with the topic of freeways several activities were carried out: (1) students in small groups using parent volunteers took Saturday exploration car trips of the entire Milwaukee freeway system, (2) maps of the current and proposed freeway system were obtained and analyzed and various individual students visited, examined, and reported on the proposed routes, and (3) the teacher interviewed a member of the Milwaukee Expressway Commission and the class listened to a tape recording of it.

These additional acquaintanceship activities clarified the big problem and *led* to the identification of researchable subquestions. The subquestions were:

1. How are freeways used?
   a. Who uses freeways? What types of vehicles are found on freeways?
   b. When are freeways used the most? The least?
   c. Are freeways efficient? Could they be more efficient?
2. Why are freeways used?
   a. Are freeways faster than regular streets?
   b. Are freeways safer than regular streets?
   c. What other reasons are there?
3. How expensive are freeways?
   a. How expensive is freeway construction?
   b. How expensive is freeway maintenance?
4. What problems do freeways create?
   a. What happens to houses and people who live in the paths of freeways?
   b. Do freeways encourage suburban growth? Retard urban growth?
   c. Is there a relationship between increasing air pollution and freeways?
   d. Is the freeway a wise use of land in metropolitan areas? What happens to parks, playgrounds, and recreational areas in the paths of freeways?
5. Is the local freeway situation unique or are other cities experiencing the same situation?

A great variety of data-gathering activities were employed, most of which were firsthand experiences. To collect information concerning the first subquestion the class observed the freeway in actual use and constructed and distributed questionnaires concerning its use. Their observation consisted of making frequency counts from a vantage point overlooking a segment of the freeway. The number and types of cars, trucks, buses, and other vehicles that passed in both directions at various times during the day and on various days of the week were recorded. Also, license plates and number of occupants in each vehicle were recorded. These data were then compared with similar counts of traffic on nearby arterial streets parallel to the freeway. The questionnaires which elicited responses concerning frequency and purpose of freeway use were distributed to a sample of suburban and inner-city parents.

Data relative to the second subquestion were obtained by an experiment, interviews, and record analysis. The experiment had to do with freeway speed. Several students had their fathers drive from a point in the suburbs to a point in the center of the city during a rush period and during a nonrush period, one car using the freeway and the other using a nonfreeway route. Departure and arrival times were recorded and compared. The interviews were with a local helicopter traffic reporter concerning freeway speed and safety and with a group of parents concerning why they do or do not use the freeway system. The traffic reporter interview was conducted over the telephone and amplified using the classroom public address system. The record analysis consisted of examining the County Sheriff's Department traffic accident records on freeways as well as on other streets. Freeway and nonfreeway safety records in relation to number of motorists and types of accidents, time of day, and type of vehicle, were compared.

The third subquestion was also answered through analysis of records. Data concerning freeway construction and maintenance costs were obtained from the Milwaukee County Expressway Commission and compared with similar data for nonfreeway highways from the Milwaukee County Highway Department.

To provide information for the fourth subquestion more interviews and questionnaires were employed. A representative from the Milwaukee City Housing Authority was interviewed by a student teacher and two students relative to relocation of families who live in the path of freeways. The interview was tape-recorded and played back to the class. A representative from the Milwaukee County Air Pollution Control Department was interviewed in class concerning air pollution from freeway traffic. Questionnaires were sent to a sample of people who were forced to move for freeway construction or who may be forced to move for future freeway construction. Views on compensation, inconvenience, and other matters were obtained. Questionnaires were also sent to a sample of suburban families inquiring about the effects freeways have had on their decision to live in a suburb.

Data for the last subquestion were obtained mainly by writing letters. Letters were written to the Secretary of Transportation, the Director of Federal Bureau of Public Roads, the Wisconsin Engineer for Public Roads, and the Chairman of the State Highway Commission. Also, letters were written to the transit authorities of Chicago, Boston, San Francisco, and other cities. Data relative to freeways in other countries were obtained by presentations from university and high school foreign students.

In organizing the collected data and composing an answer to the big question the concepts of scarcity, marginality, space, time, linkage, and others were used. The study was completed with the writing of a report by a group of five students. Study or inquiry such as this which can emerge from games and case studies requires and develops student independence, self-assurance, and responsibility. It results in instruction and classroom activity that is consonant with the goals of humanism.

This particular example of study followed the study model rather closely. Often in study the elements do not occur in this order. Sometimes not all of them are employed. The model should be viewed as a general guide and altered to meet specific situations involving knowledge problems or involving decision-action problems. Chapter 8 presents an example of an adaptation of the model concerning an action problem and discusses a variety of action techniques.

Notes

1. H. Millard Clements, William R. Fielder, and B. Robert Tabachnick, *Social Study: Inquiry in Elementary Classrooms* (New York: The Bobbs-Merrill Company, Inc., 1966).
2. *Ibid.*, p. 22.

Social Action Activities

CHAPTER 8

Throughout this book we have supported the view that social learnings related to man's achievements and problems wherever they occur in the life of the elementary school student are the proper concern of those interested in more humanistic instruction.

Thus far our attention has been focused mainly on the classroom as a center for the following activities: *simulating* social processes and problems that characterize the larger society outside the classroom—in the school as a whole and in the community outside of the school, and also *studying* knowledge problems that emerge from the simulation activities. *Planning* or weighing alternative strategies for dealing with problems in the larger society and *evaluating* what happens after strategies have been initiated have only been dealt with incidentally. While being involved in the processes of simulating, studying, planning, and evaluating, students are urged to honestly relate and clarify their own feelings. In this respect, our strategies have supported a good deal of introspection on the student's part.

The term *social action activities* refers to activities designed to effect or realize action in the school as a whole or the community outside of the school. Therefore, social action activities *in the classroom* are primarily confined to *planning* and *evaluating* as discussed in the previous paragraph.

Most important social action activities occur in the school as a whole and the community outside of the school. These areas are the "testing grounds" for ideas planned in the classroom. Our rationale for the involvement of students in such activities is clearly consistent with democratic rhetoric concerning an involved citizenry. Our belief that social action activities should be an integral part of social education is based on the assumption that one of our society's main problems is an apathetic citizenry. If our strategies for implementing humanistic instruction did not include social action activities, we would simply be adding to the problem. As most of us know by looking at our own lives, we need more than information and the "right" attitude to make our society a better one. We need to be involved in making necessary changes and supporting that which is still worth conserving.* Such involvement depends on experience or practice, for experience gives the individual the feeling that he can make a difference. Furthermore, one learns through experience the techniques needed for implementing his ideas. It is our view that this experience should be provided at an early age by our schools.

The following case study demonstrates our views on what the relationship between information, attitudes, and social action activities should be in creating a more humanistic environment.

As a result of past experiences with her third graders, a teacher felt her students would benefit from learning about the concept *power* and two subconcepts of power: *authority* and *influence*. She defined power as getting other people to do what you want them to do. Authority was defined as power given to someone or some group by law or formal agreement, such as the police have the authority to give tickets for speeding and some children are given authority by their parents to care for the family dog. Influence was defined as power not given to you but instead earned by getting other people (often those with authority) to agree that you deserve it (or at least have it), such as getting a brother or sister to help a child clean his room.

The teacher waited for the favorable moment to introduce the three concepts. It occurred when a critical incident took place in the neighborhood. Immediately after hearing about the incident, the teacher introduced the concepts of power, authority, and influence. The class participated in a Gestalt game focusing on *ways to get others to do what you want them to do* (defined as *power*).**

The class discussed weekly allowances. All students said they received one. Most students received the allowance from their fathers. The power to give an allowance was discussed and identified as *authority*. Students were asked if they had anything to say about how much money they received as an allowance. Most said no, but one boy indicated he had his allowance raised from twenty-five cents to thirty-five cents a week. The teacher pursued his comment. The student said that he told his father that his friends got thirty-five cents a week and he should too. This action on the part of the student who had his allowance raised was identified as one form of *influence*.

---

*Our definition of social action activities is broad enough in scope to include activities designed to *conserve* and *change* elements of the status quo. We do not, therefore, use the terms *social action* and *social change* synonymously.

**We hasten to add that it is often advantageous not to use role playing or case studies but rather move directly into social action activities.

The teacher then had two students participate in a role-playing situation. One student played the role of a father who had already given his daughter her thirty-five cent allowance for the week. A second girl played the role of a daughter who had recently seen a Barbi doll that she wanted to buy even though she had spent her allowance and not saved previous allowance money. The setting for the discussion between father and daughter was identified as the family living room. The following dialogue, completely extemporaneous, ensued:

Dad: Hi!

Daughter: Hi Dad! Guess what I saw today? A BARBIE DOLL!!!

Dad: Really. I thought you already had one.

Daughter: Not like this one. She's so cute and cuddly. I'd like to buy her.

Dad: Go ahead. You've saved your allowance money, haven't you?

Daughter: I already spent it. (Starts to cry.)

Dad: Well, maybe we'll go down and at least see the doll. But please stop crying.

The role-playing episode prompted the students to discuss a number of ways they try to influence their parents. The class also discussed other people and groups with authority and different ways they are influenced.

After two days of these activities (approximately forty-five minutes per day), the teacher had one student introduce the critical incident that had taken place in the neighborhood. Adjacent to the school was a pumpkin patch owned by a third-grade student's friend—an older man in the community. Fifth and sixth graders walked through the pumpkin patch each day after school often breaking the pumpkins by throwing them and kicking them.

The class decided this was an important problem they wanted to solve. The teacher then asked for suggestions as to how to solve the problem. An immediate response was to tell the principal to kick the bad kids (those who broke pumpkins) out of school. "Use his *authority!*" one student shouted.

The teacher wanted her students to experiment with a variety of ways of influencing fifth and sixth graders, with more authoritarian directives by the principal used as a last resort. She informed the principal of her objectives and he decided to let her class have time to test their social action activities.

The class decided they would like more information before they acted. They identified key subquestions which in turn one student raised in an interview with the owner of the pumpkin patch. This information was related to the class the following day.

The third-grade students then *planned* different ways of trying to influence the fifth and sixth graders. The following suggestions were made:

1. Make posters to be placed in strategic locations in the school.
2. Ask the principal for use of the public address system to communicate with older students.
3. Volunteer to speak in classes in the school about the problem.
4. Get the owner of the pumpkin patch to write an open letter to all students which would be duplicated and distributed throughout the school.

With guidance from the teacher, students formed four committees with each committee responsible for one of the tasks listed above. The teacher wanted students to realize the power of the media (posters, public address system, and the open letter) and in the process become more articulate in presenting their views to others. These objectives were met as indicated by student responses in class.

The immediate result of third graders using their influence was that fifth and sixth graders involved in breaking pumpkins said they were going to "bust up" the third graders if they did not stop their campaign. Consequently, the third-grade class decided that the teacher should take the problem directly to the principal for action. The students had learned the valuable lesson that influence only goes so far in getting others to do what you want them to do. At this point the teacher tried to inject optimism into the situation by noting how much the students had learned in the last few days.

In summary, the teacher had integrated conceptual learning, valuing, and social action activities. Let us now turn to a discussion of particular social action activities that facilitate action problems resulting from Gestalt game and case study approaches described earlier in this section of the book.

Interviews provide additional information, give the students more of a feeling for the subject of study, and help sharpen students' communication skills. Additional information is usually of a testimonial nature and as such gives children an opportunity to weigh this kind of data. Empathy with the person interviewed can prompt students into greater involvement in social action activities, and, perhaps of greater importance, students learn to be more articulate by organizing questions to pose and data gathered while at the same time practicing the communication of their ideas to others.

Interviews may occur in the classroom or on location. In both cases, a tape recording of the interview is often valuable for future reference. Some schools also have video-tape equipment that can be used on occasion.

The person being interviewed sometimes adjusts his views after interacting with the questioner. The interviewing process forces him to re-examine his views in a public forum. An adjustment in his views may in turn change his behavior. Of course, the same thing may be said for students' views and actions.

Debates and panel discussions featuring parties interested in a controversy may also be used to prompt further social action. In our judgment, however, participants are usually less likely to alter their views in a confrontation situation as contrasted to a less threatening interview situation. The main advantage of confrontation situations is that students, realizing the controversial nature of the subject, can be motivated to become more involved.

Photographs, slides, and movies created by students themselves can be effective in eliciting social action. The main advantage in having students involved in this kind of activity is that they shape the content of the presentation themselves. For example, one fourth-grade class identified the main sources of pollution in the area, took pictures of these sources with Instamatic cameras, and wrote accompanying script. They then showed their slides in class, at a school assembly, and at meetings of local civic groups.

Posters provide a good medium for influencing the actions of people in the school and community. Art work can draw the attention of the viewer to a message suggesting particular kinds of social action. Some teachers have poster contests hoping to motivate students to make better posters. Often frequented places, such as supermarkets and laundromats, are strategic locations for posters.

Poetry has recently come into vogue in many schools primarily because of attention given minority groups in general and black Americans in particular. When focused on important issues facing our nation, poetry can effectively urge social action designed to make a better society. Some teachers have had special success in tape recording poetry reading. In this way, students can improve their ability to communicate effectively by hearing their own voices as well as those of others. Self-concepts can be enhanced in the process.

Public address systems in schools afford students an excellent opportunity for communicating their ideas with respect to social action. In the process, students should learn how powerful this medium can be in reaching a large number of people in a short period of time. Secondly, they should learn that taking the offensive via the public address system gives them a strategic advantage in influencing people. Comparisons between this medium and other media, such as television and radio, should be made in evaluation sessions in class.

Bulletin boards urging different kinds of social action can catch the attention of viewers. They can also be used for logistical purposes such as announcing planning meetings for social action projects. As with many other instruments for social action, students can study traffic patterns in the school and community in order to see where the most strategic locations for the placement of bulletin boards are.

Dramatic presentations can effectively focus attention on problems requiring social action. Students can write their own skits or plays which they can then present, following the script rather closely, or they can act extemporaneously in reaction to a theme or problem. In both cases, student involvement serves as a motivating force in other social action activities. Children can also present puppet shows of a planned or extemporaneous nature. Pollution, intergroup relations, and other similar topics can provide the subject matter for presentations.

Musical compositions can be an effective vehicle for social action views. Students may decide to write their own songs or they can supply their own words to familiar melodies. Or they may wish to sing well-known songs with a social message. The 1960's and 1970's have been marked by popular groups singing songs with social action content. *We Shall Overcome* is but one example. Teachers may also wish to use dance as an expression of appropriate social action prescribed.

Letters to appropriate people and groups have served as a traditional mode of social action. Politicians, businessmen, and newspaper editors are common targets for letters. Students can also write letters to the school newsletter editor—most newsletters emanating from the superintendent's office. Students should be aware of the fact that regular form letters will probably be sent in response to their letters unless they ask questions requiring more individualized responses.

Radio and television occasionally cover school events. For example, social action activities focusing on pollution and its ill effects have received a good deal of attention on radio and television. At other times, teachers may initiate contact with radio and television stations so that children can appear on special programs. The obvious advantage of social action activities involving radio and television is widespread coverage and therefore dissemination of ideas. It is the only contact some people have with the schools.

SOCIAL ACTION ACTIVITIES   151

Student newspapers, often the result of spirit-duplicating machines, give students an excellent opportunity to express their ideas and influence the thoughts and actions of others. Such dittoed newspapers sometimes take the simple form of one or two page circulars. When organized along thematic lines, newspapers can definitely contain important social action messages. Furthermore, a variety of types of expression, such as poetry, short stories, and interviews, can be included in a student newspaper. As with other media, students who participate can gain a good deal of self-confidence and enhance their self-concepts.

Door to door interaction is an especially good way for students to become acquainted with a variety of points of view, and in the process become more articulate in expressing their own views. Some older elementary students have distributed one page sheets of paper listing major brands of detergents with a breakdown on the pollutants they contain. Other students have collected newspapers and cans for recycling. Students have also visited local stores with information on how to minimize pollution.

Parent conferences and committees can serve as common ground for social action activities. Teachers, students, and their parents have an opportunity to express their views and plan appropriate action.

In conclusion, social action activities as well as studying knowledge problems should in our view be integrated with Gestalt game and case study approaches described in previous chapters. These strategies result in a teaching-learning process and content that helps students to become informed, empathic, active, and responsible individuals, or, in short, more humane individuals who may create a more humane world.

Appendix

Additional Gestalt Games

BACK TO NATURE
(Urbanization)

OBJECTIVES: As a result of this lesson, students should be able to:
1. Indicate how indiscriminate lumbering and building affects the quality of our existence.
2. Identify several reasons for indiscriminate lumbering and building affecting the quality of our existence.
3. Identify short and long range consequences of this practice.

METHODS AND MATERIALS:
1. Announce to the class that a land development company has acquired an option on a large tract of forest land in a northern community. If the developer can get building restrictions changed, he will cut down the trees and build a recreation area in conjunction with an apartment complex.
2. Inform students that a group is organizing to fight the development. Have the class form four groups:
   a. The representative of the developer.
   b. The residents of the area that support the developer.
   c. The residents of the area who are against the developer.
   d. A national group interested in ecology—the group being against the development.
3. After giving the students time to form coalitions and build their cases, announce that the class will now pretend it is at city hall for a hearing on the subject-at-hand. Having one student act as the moderator, let the individuals who wish to present their views.
4. Discuss the arguments for and against development. (If students have not brought out the distinction between short range and long range consequences, introduce the distinction and continue the discussion.)
5. Invite a representative from the mayor's office into class or have a few student volunteers interview him at city hall concerning how this kind of issue would be resolved if it occurred in your community.

EVALUATION:
   Observation of student views and participation in role playing and discussion.

COMMUTER ATTITUDES
(Urbanization)

OBJECTIVES: As a result of this lesson, students should be able to:
1. Suggest advantages and disadvantages of being a commuter and of being an urban dweller.
2. Conclude that where one lives—his residence—may influence what he values.
3. Understand that the influence that people exert is based on their belief systems.
4. Conclude that decision-making is difficult and complex.

METHODS AND MATERIALS:
1. Announce to the class that a mayor of a large city, about the size of Milwaukee, is going to meet with representatives of two different groups concerning a controversial issue. *The issue is whether or not commuters should be allowed to use city facilities such as the public library without a nominal fee.* The fee can be paid in one of two ways: each person who enters the library pays 50 cents, or the place of residence (suburban city hall) will be charged 50 cents per book checked out with funds for this coming from tax money collected in the suburb.
2. Choose one person to be the mayor. Have the remainder of the class form two groups, one representing the commuters and the other representing the city dwellers. Have one group sit on one side of the room and the other group sit on the opposite side with the mayor in the middle.
3. Give each side 10 minutes to talk to the mayor with the other side remaining quiet. Then let the sides debate with each other in front of the mayor for 10 minutes.
4. Have the sides change roles for a brief time if they wish.
5. Inform the mayor before class that he should not make a final decision at this time but ask sides to get more information.
6. Discuss issues and resultant problems.
7. Have a representative of the city's office of the mayor and a similar representative from a suburb visit the class and/or have small group of student volunteers tape-record interviews at respective community offices and replay recording for entire class.

EVALUATION:
   Observe pupil responses during role playing and discussion.

LOYALTY TO COMMUNITY
(Urbanization)

OBJECTIVES: As a result of this lesson, students should be able to:
1. Define the concept community.
2. Observe that people feel loyal to their community in the face of some outside pressure or common disaster.
3. Recognize that some form of cooperation may be necessary to solve a common problem.

METHODS AND MATERIALS:
1. Have students pretend that they are all members of a suburban neighborhood. They all live in beautiful homes with well-kept yards. Most of them rarely associate with anyone other than their immediate next-door neighbor.
2. They have just been informed that the freeway will cut through their neighborhood making the street in front of their homes a main thoroughfare. Up until now the only traffic on the street has been from residents and their friends. Now the heavy traffic will make the neighborhood noisy and dangerous for child play.
3. The only way that they can do anything to protect their neighborhood is through group action because city hall will only listen to them as a group.
4. They are to do everything to prevent the freeway from ruining their neighborhood.
5. Discuss the role-playing session. Some possible questions are:
   a. How did you feel when you first learned that the freeway was going through your neighborhood?
   b. How did it affect your relationship with your neighbors?

EVALUATION:
Observe students during role playing and discussion.

CITY KNOWLEDGE, RURAL KNOWLEDGE
(Urbanization)

OBJECTIVES: As a result of this lesson, students should be able to:
1. List reasons for standardizing road signs.
2. Relate feelings concerning what it is like not to know what a sign means.

METHODS AND MATERIALS:
1. Divide the class into two volunteer groups as nearly equal in number as possible.
2. Announce that each group will pretend they are driving in a rural area such as .... (a nearby area known to the students).

3. Show one group standardized signs with which they are already familiar—e.g., stop sign, railroad sign, parking sign, etc.
4. Show the second group signs with totally different symbols which correspond with the first group's signs—e.g., Δ = stop sign, $\square$ = railroad sign, $\square\!\!\!/$ = parking sign, etc.
5. Have each group discuss the role playing. Possible discussion questions are:
   a. What did it feel like to take a drive and recognize or not recognize the signs?
   b. Is it important to be able to recognize what each sign means immediately? Why?
   c. Can you name anything in America that was not changed by the automobile?
   d. Since both the city and country were changed by the automobile, why is it important that signs be standardized?

EVALUATION:
Observation of class discussion.

TROUBLE IN SCHOOLS
(Urbanization)

OBJECTIVES: As a result of this lesson, students should be able to:
1. Identify inequality of facilities in a school system as a source of trouble in the schools.
2. Identify language not familiar to the students as a source of trouble in the schools.

METHODS AND MATERIALS:
1. Divide the class into three volunteer groups. Have one group put their desks into a large area. If possible, put an interesting decoration in their area. Make sure everyone has paper and pencil and an appropriate book to use for some short activity. An example might be a dictionary exercise. Tell them that when they are done, they may read, have some candy, or play a game.
2. Put the second group in an area with enough room for the desks and give the students the same activity to do with the appropriate books, but do not offer them a reward for accomplishing the activity.
3. Put the third group in a small area. Give them the same task to do, but do not give each student a book to use or enough pencils and paper. Have them share their resources. Give them directions in Pig Latin or a foreign language and do not repeat instructions if they did not understand. Do not provide a reward for the completion of the task, but threaten them with punishment if they do not get done in the same time as the other groups.

4. After the first two groups have finished their activities, discuss the episodes. Ask how they would feel working under those conditions all of the time. Particularly ask those who were in the third group how they felt knowing that there were better conditions available. Also, discuss the problem they might have had of not being able to understand all the directions that were given in Pig Latin.

(For another activity have someone who is fluent in a foreign language present a short lesson to the class in that language. Then have the students discuss how they felt about getting all their instruction in a different language. Help the students identify groups of students that might be working under such a handicap.)

EVALUATION:
Observe class activities and discussion.

VOCATIONS: POVERTY
(Technological Change)

OBJECTIVES: As a result of this lesson, students should be able to:
1. Describe poverty, e.g., what it feels like to be poor.
2. Differentiate between what society defines as lower or higher status occupations, and how the worker feels in each job.

METHODS AND MATERIALS:
1. The class should be told that they will be playing a game about occupations. Two students will be "workers."
2. The students will arrange their desks in a circle. Two chairs will face the back of the room. The two workers will occupy these chairs. Two "stores" will be set up in the front of the room. (The teacher's desk may serve this purpose.) One store will have a plate of assorted cookies with a one cent price tag. The other store will have a plate of only one kind of cookies and a two cent price tag. (This should be set up without the knowledge of the two workers.) The teacher will need three price signs, two plates of cookies, and ten poker chips.
3. The two workers will each be assigned a task for which they will be paid after three minutes of work. One student will be told to write an eviction notice. The other student will be told to spend the three minutes transferring his books from the desk to the floor and back. After the three minutes the students will be paid. The manual laborer will get one chip and the clerk will get two chips. Each will then be able to spend their chips at the store. The manual laborer may only buy from the two cent store. The clerk will shop at the one cent store.
4. The manual laborer will then be given the opportunity to earn more money to buy a cookie (the clerk will be given the same

opportunity). After the two workers start their next work period, the teacher will raise the price in the manual laborer's store to three cents. The price in the clerk's store will remain the same. Upon completion of the task, the workers will receive the same pay that they got for the first job.
5. Each worker should be asked to describe their feelings in the role that each played. A discussion may then be conducted on what it feels like to be poor and what it means to hold a high or a low status job.

EVALUATION:

Student discussion or students may also be asked to write a few paragraphs on what is poverty or some other related topics that emerged.

TECHNOLOGICAL UNEMPLOYMENT
(Technological Change)

OBJECTIVES: As a result of this lesson, students should be able to:
1. Define unemployment.
2. Recognize that technological unemployment occurs regardless of the efforts of the individual who has been displaced.
3. Identify feelings the technologically unemployed may have, such as feelings of frustration and failure.

METHODS AND MATERIALS:
1. The teacher will distribute sheets of paper to all the students explaining that squares of paper two inches by two inches are needed. Each student is to make as many squares as possible using no scissors or ruler, but only folding and tearing.
2. For every two squares of paper made the student will be rewarded, for example, with a jelly bean. The number of squares and type of reward is unimportant.
3. The teacher then allows a small number of selected students to use scissors, ruler, and pencil to make neater and more accurate squares.
4. The teacher begins to reject the squares that are folded and torn as not being as good as the measured and cut squares, but she does not allow those who fold to use the scissors.
5. After this activity has gone on long enough to build up a level of vocal frustration, a discussion should be started. Questions such as the following should be discussed:
    a. How did they feel about not being able to earn any more jelly beans?
    b. How did those people who were allowed to use scissors feel about the other students? Were they concerned for them or were they glad that they were not being rewarded?

APPENDIX—ADDITIONAL GESTALT GAMES

    c. What does unemployment mean to you?
    d. How can people lose jobs because there are newer, faster ways of doing things?
    e. How would you define technological unemployment?
    f. What can the people who are unemployed because of changes in technology do about it?
    g. What can the students do in this situation?
    (The teacher should be prepared to point out several examples of machines replacing people at jobs. A simple example readily understood by students would be the use of automatic harvesting machines replacing workers in the fields.)

EVALUATION:
Observation of discussion or have the students write their own definitions of unemployment and ways in which a person can lose his job because of technological change.

INFLUENCING THE MEDIA
(Technological Change)

OBJECTIVES: As a result of this lesson, students should be able to:
1. Identify difficulties in accurate reporting.
2. Describe problems of selecting items to be covered in the media.
3. Write a short story for a news report.

METHODS AND MATERIALS:
1. Problems of observation.
    a. Have the class form into groups of five or seven students. Tell the student groups to divide themselves further into two equal sections with one student left out to act as a reporter. One section of two or three students should present a two-minute impromptu activity for the one reporter student without the other section of two or three students watching. Then, tell the reporter student to tell the others what happened. They in turn should report back to the pupils who did the acting to assess how accurate their understanding was of what happened.
    b. Bring the class back together to discuss the question of accuracy of reporting.
2. Problems of selecting material to be covered by the media.
    a. Designate three volunteers as editors. Divide the rest of the class into groups of threes or fours. Give the groups time to devise a short skit or activity to act out. Tell the editors that they are responsible for putting together a news report for that day's happenings but they are limited in the number of things they can cover to at least two stories less than the number of groups into which the class is divided. Ask the groups to start their performances and let the editors observe

the activities. Give the editors a few minutes to confer with each other about their selection of activities to include in the news report and then have them report to the class about which activities they chose and why they chose them.
   b. Discuss why the choices were made and what the class thinks about those choices. Find out how those people felt whose activity was not chosen. It would be useful to discuss with the class the fact that every news covering organization must limit the amount of information it carries and that each newspaper or broadcast media works out its own rules for which events to report.
3. Involvement with the media—activity suggestions.
   a. The students could put together a classroom newspaper and/or taped radio news broadcast using the events from the classroom or information from students' homes.
   b. The students could collect news items from other teachers and classes and prepare a school newspaper or provide several news spots for the school announcements over the PA system.
   c. Field trips could be arranged to local newspapers and television or radio stations. If possible, the students could write an article or news report on an activity and have it printed in the local newspaper.
   d. The class should be introduced to the letters to the editor column in the newspaper. After a discussion on an issue of interest to the students, the members of the class could write letters to the local newspaper.

EVALUATION:
Observe class response and evaluate the written items discussed.

AIR POLLUTION
(Survival)

OBJECTIVES: As a result of this lesson, students should be able to:
1. Indicate that air pollution can annoy or bother many people.
2. Indicate that group action may be essential to prevent air pollution.

METHODS AND MATERIALS:
1. Before the class begins the teacher should identify several student volunteers. These students should each be given a spray can of aerosol room freshener with instructions to spray some of it into the air every few minutes. When the class is started at their usual activities, the children with the spray cans should begin to spray.
2. When the class questions the activities of the sprayers, the teacher should say that today there is no class rule against room fresheners.

3. After a short time, the class should begin to complain bitterly about the smell.
4. When this has gone far enough, a discussion of the problem should begin. The discussion can start with the following question: Today air spraying is permitted because companies and villages and cities pollute the air that everyone breathes, therefore what is wrong with polluting the air in the class?
Later the discussion can turn to what the students want to do about the situation.
A possible solution might be for the students to decide to make up class rules for themselves that such sprays not be allowed.

EVALUATION:
Observation of class discussion.

OVERCROWDED TERRITORY
(Survival)

OBJECTIVES: As a result of this lesson, students should be able to:
1. Indicate their views as to what happened to them emotionally and physically when they occupied an overcrowded territory as contrasted to an open-spaced territory.
2. Conclude that space relationships between people in different territories vary from territory to territory.

METHODS AND MATERIALS:
1. Before the class begins, block off 3 areas in the classroom. Select 8 volunteers to move their desks into the smallest area. Select 8 different volunteers to move their desks into an area about half again as big as the smallest area. The remainder of the students will spread their desks about the remaining space.
2. Explain to each group that they may move about their area, but may not extend area boundaries.
3. Resume classroom sessions as usual with the students remaining in their areas for at least 3 days.
4. After 3 days, have the groups move to different sized areas than previously occupied—preferably having the majority experiencing the extremes.
5. Initiate a discussion with a question such as the following:
How did *physical restrictions in the various territories affect your attitudes and feelings* toward each other and your work?
6. Show and discuss pictures for magazines depicting living conditions in different territories in the United States and other countries.

EVALUATION:
Observe individual and group responses during the discussion.

RECYCLING CANS AND PAPER
(Survival)

OBJECTIVES: As a result of this lesson, students should be able to:
1. Describe and demonstrate many personal ways of recycling and reusing various waste products.
2. Describe ways that the community or the society could recycle waste.

METHODS AND MATERIALS:
1. Place on display some garbage items from home and school (cans, bottles, newspapers, rags, bottle caps, plastic bottles, gum wrappers, soda straws, various bits of paper). Also display items that can be made from garbage (papier-maché objects, an odds and ends rack made from discarded jars and/or cans, a vase made of a papier-maché covered bottle, a bottle cap welcome mat, rag potholders, a rag rug, soda straw curtains, 'found' art collage).
2. Discuss garbage and waste and the objects and how they were made. Discuss waste problems (what to do with it, running out of dump sights, burning and air pollution). Select three garbage items and discuss what could be done with these items (a soda can, an old brick, a piece of scrap cloth, etc.).
   Invite students to bring an item or two from home that would ordinarily have been thrown out and engage in projects, either group or individual, using these objects so that they are recycled. Display reused articles.
3. Discuss what items can and cannot be recycled by individuals and how items can be recycled.

EVALUATION:
Observe responses during discussion and reports on reusable waste, models, and exhibits of waste.

INFORMATION SUMMARIZING
(Survival)

OBJECTIVES: As a result of this lesson, students should be able to:
1. Realize that interpretations result from such factors as personal biases, personal background, and personal opinions and attitudes.
2. Conclude that it is valuable to scrutinize content of communication media in order to ascertain objectivity and validity.

METHODS AND MATERIALS:
1. Choose three volunteers to act as newspaper reporters, one being a young Black reporter for a Black community newspaper, one being a young student reporter for a reputed radical college publication, and the last one being a white, middle-aged reporter for a large city publication.

APPENDIX—ADDITIONAL GESTALT GAMES

2. Select a student to act as a police officer in a large city. Have three other students act as college demonstrators refusing to move from an entrance they are blocking.
3. Have the police officers and the students confront one another while the reporters observe.
4. Have the reporters, each mindful of his position and personal background, relate his "story" of the incident to the remainder of the class, who also observed the confrontation.
5. Discuss the three stories; analyze their similarities and differences (reasons behind each one's interpretations).

EVALUATION:
Observe student responses and questions during the discussion.

NOISE POLLUTION
(Survival)

OBJECTIVES: As a result of this lesson, students should be able to:
1. Define noise pollution.
2. State why noise pollution can be harmful and in what ways it is harmful.
3. Indicate some ways of dealing with noise pollution on the personal level (in the home and school).

METHODS AND MATERIALS:
1. Select five volunteers to act as noisemakers. They should be scatterd in their regular places through the room. One should drum regularly with his pencil on the desk. Two should, after a little while, drum louder and irregularly on the metal part of the desk. Then three and four should start talking loudly. Then five should make crashing noises—dropping his books and other objects on the floor.
2. After these five are briefed, engage the class in an activity that requires silence and concentration. When the class is started, have the noisemakers start.
3. After the crash discuss the reactions of the class and what other kinds of noise pollution they have experienced.
4. Discuss blocked noises (noises you normally don't choose to hear), noise pollution, the dangers of noise pollution, and what can be done to stop it.
5. Invite students to, in writing, define noise pollution, tell why it is harmful, and what they can do to stop it.

EVALUATION:
Observe responses in the discussion, and in the written work.

WATER POLLUTION
(Survival)

OBJECTIVES: As a result of this lesson, students should be able to:
1. Describe what water pollution is.
2. Identify some of its causes.
3. Relate water pollution effects on resident animals and/or plants.
4. Identify positive alternatives for solution to water pollution problem.

METHODS AND MATERIALS:
1. Prepare two, large, well-balanced aquaria with some type of tropical fish and snails, placing them side by side within the classroom.
2. Inform class that, for Aquarium A, only the correctly prescribed amount of fish food is to be given daily; and no other elements are to be added to the water.
3. For Aquarium B, students may give fish as much food as they wish, feeding them as often as they care to. In addition, any items that students would normally throw away in classroom wastebasket may, if so desired, be deposited in Aquarium B.
4. Observe over period of time what happens to animals and plants living in Aquaria A and B, respectively.
5. Discuss effects of differential treatment to two aquaria. Observe individual and group conclusions in discussion.
   Possible discussion questions are:
   a. What is water pollution?
   b. What are some of its causes?
   c. What positive steps can be taken to alleviate water pollution?
   d. How might the study of these aquaria be compared (generalized) to our lake and river problems?

EVALUATION:
Observe student comments during discussion of the two treatments.

POSITIVE REINFORCERS: SMILES AND NODS
(Intergroup Relations)

OBJECTIVES: As a result of this lesson, students should be able to:
1. Demonstrate that they have paid attention to positive and negative gestures used by fellow classmates.
2. Observe the effects gestures have on other people.
3. Distinguish between positive and negative gestures.
4. Relate examples of positive and negative gestures.

METHODS AND MATERIALS:
1. Have pupils form a circle with their desks or chairs.
2. Ask them to sit silently and look at the person sitting directly opposite them—have them remain in such a manner for 3 minutes.
3. Randomly select several pupils and ask them what happened during the last 3 minutes—lead discussion to specific features they noticed in their partner and list on blackboard.
4. Repeat procedure but let pupils mingle freely about the room. Give them one instruction: OBSERVE. Tally responses on blackboard.
5. Students should be curious by now. Discuss topic *gestures* with special emphasis on smiles and nods. Ask how they were affected by smiles and nods as contrasted to negative responses such as frowns.
6. Have student from another class in school give a report and ask pupils to observe his/her gestures, both positive and negative, after which discussion will occur.
7. Have students bring in pictures from newspapers and magazines demonstrating the importance of positive and negative gestures.
8. Have students select topics emphasizing positive and negative gestures and have them present them using pantomimes.

EVALUATION:
Pupil responses should be observed—both verbal and nonverbal.

PREFERENTIAL TREATMENT
(Intergroup Relations)

OBJECTIVES: As a result of this lesson, students should be able to:
1. Define social injustice.
2. Identify some of the feelings of people who are victims of social injustice.
3. Identify the roles of those people concerned with social injustice.

METHODS AND MATERIALS:
1. Give all students, except one volunteer, bags containing jelly beans. Some bags should contain only 5 jelly beans and a label, "poor man." Other bags should contain 10 jelly beans and a label, "rich man." Tell the students with the "rich man" labels that they will be permitted to take the jelly beans from the "poor man" labelled students although they may take no more than one jelly bean at a time. No students should be allowed to eat the jelly beans until the session is over.
2. Give the one student without a bag of jelly beans a label reading CONSCIENCE. Tell him that he should speak out about the activities of the "rich man" students.

3. After the activities have continued long enough so that the "poor man" students have no jelly beans left, have the class discuss such questions as what were the feelings of the "poor man" students as they had to give up their jelly beans, what were the feelings of the "rich man" students, and what were their feelings about CONSCIENCE.

EVALUATION:

Observe student behavior during role-playing session and class discussion.

POSITIVE REINFORCERS: COMMENTS
(Intergroup Relations)

OBJECTIVES: As a result of this lesson, students should be able to:
1. Recognize that people usually respond more favorably to a positive comment than a negative one.
2. Identify with the feelings of those who receive a negative comment and those who receive a positive comment.

METHODS AND MATERIALS:
1. Several incidents should be acted out in the classroom.
   One incident will show one student bumping into another. The student will not say "I am sorry," but will criticize the other person for being in his way.
   The same incident will be repeated, this time the student will say "I am sorry" and go on his way.
2. Another incident to be acted out will show one student walking by another student's desk. He knocks down a book and refuses to pick it up. A fight results.
   The same incident is repeated. This time the student who knocked the book down picks it up and says that he is sorry. After these incidents a group discussion should be held.
3. Discuss the incidents. Possible questions are:
   a. How do you think the person felt who was bumped into and accused of being in the way, or the student whose book was knocked on the floor and not picked up? Do you think they felt good or bad? Why?
   b. How do you think the people who were rude felt?
   c. What does it feel like to say that you are sorry or apologize for something you do? How does the other person feel?

EVALUATION:
1. Observation of the class discussion.
2. Observation of later behavior in regard to positive comments.

APPENDIX—ADDITIONAL GESTALT GAMES

POSITIVE REINFORCERS: COMMENTS
(Intergroup Relations)

OBJECTIVES: As a result of this lesson, students should be able to:
1. Demonstrate awareness of various comments used by fellow class members.
2. Observe the effects of such comments on different people.
3. Demonstrate that they can distinguish between positive and negative comments.

METHODS AND MATERIALS:
1. Identify commonly used words, such as "huh," "you know," "okay," with the class. Assign one such word to each student volunteer with the instructions that his job is to keep a tally for the next couple of days as to the number of times the word was used and the kind of response it received.
2. Discuss how many times words were used and results they achieved—effects on other people.
3. On another day ask half of the class to state all of their responses —both to teacher and fellow students—negatively—e.g., "I can't do this problem," "I don't want to," "no." Do this for about 20 minutes and then discuss tone of class. Then for the next 20 minutes have the class offer only positive comments and discuss the results.
4. Invite students to read newspapers, magazine articles, and observe television programs noting responses—both positive and negative. Discuss in class.

EVALUATION:
Observe student verbal responses and opinions.

COMPROMISING 2
(Intergroup Relations)

OBJECTIVES: As a result of this lesson students should be able to recognize that it is often necessary to compromise or to give up one thing to achieve another.

METHODS AND MATERIALS:
1. Have the class form into four groups. Tell each group that they must choose a person to run for the office of Dispenser of Candy for the room. In five minutes another member of the group should be able to tell the whole class why his group's candidate should be elected Dispenser of Candy. After each group has presented its candidate to the class, a vote will be taken. Explain that if the class is able to elect a Dispenser of Candy by more than half the

class voting for one candidate, the Dispenser of Candy will be allowed to dispense one piece of candy to each member of the class. The people who are members of the group whose candidate won the job will receive two pieces of candy. It will probably be necessary to take more than one vote and to allow some informal discussion time between the votes.
2. After the activity a discussion should be held centering around the idea that it was necessary to give up something, that is the two pieces of candy, in order to get any at all.

EVALUATION:
Observe the activities and discussion.

POPULATION
(Intergroup Relations)

OBJECTIVES: As a result of this lesson, students should be able to:
1. Compare the feelings of family members concerning the distribution of food.
2. Compare the similar and dissimilar reasons for food purchasing.

METHODS AND MATERIALS:
1. Have the class form into unequal families of from two to eight members. On index cards label the head of family, the family members, and the family size. Give each family head the same number of cookies to pass out. Have families eat the cookies.
2. Discuss the feelings of the different families when the cookies were passed out and eaten.
  Enumerate similar and dissimilar reasons families purchase food.

EVALUATION:
Invite students to write an essay about their family's food purchasing.

INTOLERANCE
(Intergroup Relations)

OBJECTIVES: As a result of this lesson, students should be able to:
1. Define intolerance.
2. Relate some of the things that people can be intolerant of (written or oral).
3. Relate at least one harmful effect of intolerance.

METHODS AND MATERIALS:
1. Along one side of the room on tables lay from 7 to 10 piles of paper. Each pile should have the same number of sheets as there are students in the room. The piles should be in a row with a stapler at each end. If possible the piles should be from one to two feet apart.

APPENDIX—ADDITIONAL GESTALT GAMES

2. Divide the room in half. One-half believes that the only way to pick up the papers and staple them into a book is to go from left to right down the row. This is because it is the only right way to pick up papers, this is the way people read and therefore is the only natural way, etc. The other half believes that the only right way to pick up the papers and staple them is to go right to left down the row. This is because any other way is stupid and because most people are right-handed and therefore it is more efficient.
3. Neither group is going to give up its ideas. If you believe you are right and all else are wrong you have to stick by your beliefs. Make sure this direction is clear to each group.
4. The whole class goes to pick up and staple their papers at the same time, each group starting at its end and going down the line.
5. Discuss what happened. Each group should give its reactions. Definitions of "Intolerance" should be attempted. What happened when groups are intolerant of others should also be discussed.

EVALUATION:
Observe the activity and the discussion.

INTOLERANCE
(Intergroup Relations)

OBJECTIVES: As a result of this lesson, students should be able to:
1. Give a working definition of intolerance.
2. Identify several examples of intolerance as it has affected people in history and today.

METHODS AND MATERIALS:
1. Have the class form two equal groups and role play the following situation:
   a. Two tribes live next to each other in the land of Ub. One is a tribe of sun god worshippers and the other is a tribe of tree spirit worshippers. The tribes have contact with each other through trade. Each tribe feels that they are worshipping the only true god and that the other tribe worships a false god and has strange and, therefore, barbaric customs. For the past year there has been a severe drought which has ruined crops and made hunting for food more difficult. The sun god worshipper priests have told their people that the drought is a punishment because the tribe has been neglecting the sun god. The tribe has a special sun stone through which they worship the sun god. The priests say that in order to appease the sun god and end the drought the tribe must build a temple to place the sun stone in. The temple must face west and it must be located in such a way that when the sun sets on

March 22 and on September 21 the sun's rays will touch the stone at a special angle. The priests have determined the right angle. They have found a place on a nearby hill for the temple. There are other places but this is the best place as far as convenience is concerned. The only obstacle is a large tree that would stand in the way of the sun's rays. If it could be cut down the temple could be easily built. It is necessary to build the temple quickly so that it is finished before September 21 and so that the drought will be ended and the tribal crops saved. The village depends mostly on crops for its living and the crops need rain to grow.

The tree spirit worshipper priests have told their people that the drought is a punishment because the tribe has been neglecting the spirits of the trees. The tribe worships spirits. These spirits help the tribe by helping the hunters find game. The tribe depends mainly on hunting for its survival. It is the duty of the tribe to find homes for the tree spirits. This is done by consecrating trees that are especially large and with many limbs. The priests have said that the drought is being caused by the tree spirit Ni who is mad because his tree is dying and the tribe has not found a new one for him. Tree consecration takes a month and is a long, involved ceremony. It takes time to find the right tree, but the priests have found one. It is on the same nearby hill that the sun god worshippers want to build their temple. The tree is the one they want to cut down.

b. Both tribes meet on the hill. Five men are selected from each tribe to discuss the situation with each other to decide what to do. Then they will meet with the other tribe. The selected men are:

Sun-Worshippers:

High Priest. He believes that their god wants the temple where they are going to place it. Furthermore he believes the other tribe to be heathens. He would like to convert them to his religion. He feels a good first step would be to destroy their gods and he sees a good way to do this is to cut down that tree, even if it means war.

Tribal Leader. He is worried by the drought. If it continues much longer he is afraid that the village may die off. He is anxious to please the gods. He also feels that the other tribe is taking up land for hunting that could be put to much better use as cropland. He would welcome a war as a way to show those heathens who has the true god and to obtain a bit more land.

Farmer. He has been hurt by the drought and will do anything to appease the sun god. If a temple will stop the drought then he will insist that the temple be built. However, he does not want war. If there was a war he and his sons would have to go to help fight and then no one would be there to take care of his farm and plant the crops. Then again, if the drought continues he would lose his land anyway.

Merchant. He does not want war, it would hurt his trade with the tree spirit worshipper tribe. He would like to avoid all the trouble and just find another location for the temple.

Old Man. He knows from experience that wars are not always the best way to solve problems. He feels the other tribe has barbaric customs and feels his tribe would be better off with little contact with their strange ways. He has seen droughts come and go before in his long life and is not particularly worried by this one.

Tree-Spirit Worshippers:

High Priest. He looked a long time before he found this tree. It is the best tree for Ni in the area. He feels nothing but contempt for the sun worshippers and their false god. He does not want their temple so close to his village. He is worried that some of the heathenish customs of the sun worshippers may be picked up by the young people in his tribe. A war to defeat the sun worshippers would stop this once and for all.

Tribal Leader. The drought has driven much of the game away. He is anxious to appease Ni and get the affairs of the village back to normal. If the drought continues much longer, much of the tribe will starve. He feels that the farmers of the other tribe are taking some of the tribe's land and scaring the same away. He feels a successful war would stop this encroachment.

Hunter. Hunting has been hard. His family is hungry. He wants to quickly please Ni and find a home for him. He feels the tribe could win a war but he is afraid that by the time everything got settled after a war many people would have starved.

Trader. He makes his living by supplying the village with many of the things they can't make. A war would ruin his trade and his living for quite a while—no matter who won. He feels one tree is as good as another.

Wise Man. He feels that Ni might be appeased into taking a lesser tree. He does not see why it has to be this one particular tree. He feels, however, that the barbaric sun worshippers should be taught a lesson. He is worried by their strange ways and their worship of an alien god.

Each group should decide which students will role play the five men.
2. Following role playing of the incident tolerance and intolerance that emerged from this situation should be discussed. Also, tolerance and intolerance in students' lives should be discussed.

EVALUATION:

Teacher observation of role play behavior and emotion, and discussion comments.

COMPROMISE 3
(Intragroup Relations)

OBJECTIVES: As a result of this lesson, students should be able to explain that it is often necessary to work with other people that all may benefit.

METHODS AND MATERIALS:
1. The teacher will distribute to the class pieces of magazine pictures that have been cut in half and instruct them to have at least one completed picture in ten minutes, although not necessarily one of the pictures they were given.
2. Depending on the size of the group it may be necessary to label the pictures as to who has the other half of the picture or letter the pictures so that the person holding the other half may be easily found.
3. The pictures should be distributed so that each student does not have a straight exchange with another student, but the pictures should be in units of three or four. Example—Student 1 has half of pictures A and C; Student 2 has half of B and D; Student 3 has half of A and B; and Student 4 has half of C and D.
4. The students should be allowed to form groups for five minutes or so to work out their exchanges and mount their pictures.
5. Then the class should discuss what they have done. Possible questions are:
    a. How was the problem of getting the other halves of the pictures solved?
    b. What would have happened if others had not been willing to pool their pictures or at least been willing to give up one of their halves for a half that did not complete a picture?
    c. How do you feel about giving up something you have or want to someone else to achieve a desired goal?

EVALUATION:

Observation of the class discussion.

APPENDIX—ADDITIONAL GESTALT GAMES

MARGINALITY: IMMIGRANTS
(Intragroup Relations)

OBJECTIVES: As a result of this lesson, students should be able to describe what nonacceptance by a group means to them and how people may react to such nonacceptance.

METHODS AND MATERIALS:
1. The teacher will divide the class into volunteer groups of three or four students, leaving a small group of students unattached to any group.
2. Each group will be put to work on a task such as practicing an unfamiliar group of vocabulary words with each student in the group participating. The task is not important and could be anything a small group could work on independently.
3. Each group will be told quietly by the teacher that they are not to admit anyone to their group unless the outsider can do whatever they are doing better than they can.
4. The unattached students then should be told to go to a group and try to join in.
5. After the activity has continued long enough for the students to get the idea, a discussion should be held. Possible questions are:
   a. How did it feel to be left out of a group and experience difficulty in being admitted to a group?
   b. How did it feel to exclude people from a group?
   c. Did anyone experience a problem in telling someone they liked that they could not join the group.

EVALUATION:
Observation of the class discussion.

CONFORMITY
(Intragroup Relations)

OBJECTIVES: As a result of this lesson, students should be able to:
1. Conclude that a group can be described by what the members have in common with one another.
2. Understand that when people adopt certain characteristics to become part of a group, they are conforming to that group. If a person does not conform he is out of the group.
3. Understand that conformity is necessary for a group's existence.
4. Conclude that conformity can have negative connotations (in situations where conformity conflicts with individual integrity.)

METHODS AND MATERIALS:
1. Select four or five volunteers to be part of a special No-Classroom Cleanup group. All members in this group will not have to do the homework cleanup work for that afternoon. To be members

of this group the students will have to do two things: they will have to hold one of their arms in a sling position and they will have to start every sentence they say or write with the word "Peacock."
2. Organize the classroom cleanup for that day. Explain that there is a special group that does not have to do the cleanup. Members of this group have things in common. Anyone may join this group, but all members of the group must follow the characteristics of the group. When a student feels he has determined the common characteristics, he may ask a member to see if he is right. If he is right and agrees to follow the group, he is then a member of the group.
3. When most students are in the No-Classroom Cleanup group, announce that it is no longer necessary to hold arms in the sling position and say "Peacock" to get out of doing cleanup work. There will be no cleanup today. Continue the free period a little longer and observe reactions. Actions should stop and group should fall apart.
4. Have students respond to the following in writing:
   a. What happened when the group was first announced?
   b. What happened when it was announced that they did not have to do anything to get out of cleanup?
   c. What happened to the group?
   d. Would you have: jumped up and down 3 times once every 5 minutes, drunk a tablespoon of cod liver oil (or medicine, cough syrup, etc.), drunk a little bit of poison (enough to get sick), told a false rumor about a friend, done 5 jumping jacks, or stolen a quarter from a friend in order to get into the group? Why or Why Not?
5. Discuss answers and the term "conformity."

EVALUATION:

Note student responses to description of a group. Observe student reactions during the conforming period with the group. Observe student responses, written and oral, during the discussion and question period.

MARGINALITY: IMMIGRANTS VS. ANGLO-SAXON AMERICANS
(Intragroup Relations)

OBJECTIVE: As a result of this lesson, students should be able to identify some problems of gaining acceptance facing immigrants to an area.

METHODS AND MATERIALS:
1. Read or distribute copies of the background information on Nova Terra to the class and then have the class form into groups of at least six to play the roles specified in the game.

APPENDIX—ADDITIONAL GESTALT GAMES 177

2. Nova Terra Game

Twenty-five years ago a spaceship from Earth carrying 750 colonists crash landed on the planet they called Nova Terra. The spaceship was bound for another planet in another part of the galaxy. The equipment on board and the plants and animals carried were chosen because they would be useful for the conditions on the other planet; they were not planned for Nova Terra. When the ship crashed, it destroyed the communications system and the engines, making it impossible for the people on the ship either to get off the planet or to get help from anyone else. Many of the animals carried in the ship died on Nova Terra and most of the plants were not suitable. Like the Pilgrims in America back in the history of Earth many of the colonists died in the first hard years of learning what plants would grow and of learning what they could eat that already grew on the planet. The sudden storms that swept across the planet took many lives until the people learned how to forecast the weather. Gradually the colonists have been able to build up their farms and their homes and the colony is successfully growing. The colonists have explored the planet and have discoverd that most of the planet is water with one large continent the colonists called Terra Firma and one small island called Parva.

Now the council of the colony is meeting to consider a new crisis that is facing the colony. The council is made of five people (chaplin, successful farmer, young farmer, doctor, teacher), each one representing one hundred of the present colonists. Yesterday another ship in distress landed. It is carrying 450 colonists from the settlement on Mars outbound to another planet. Although the grandparents of these people from Mars had come from Earth in the first place, the time that their families had lived on Mars had changed their language somewhat and changed their customs from those on Earth. Now the captain from the spaceship is appealing to the council for permission for the Martian colonists to settle here on Nova Terra. The communicators on the ship have been ruined, but it would be possible to fix the short range drive of the ship, but not the engines that could carry it across the galaxy. If the short range drive is fixed and the ship is able to lift off, the problem is that nothing is known of the area of the galaxy. No one on Nova Terra knows whether there is another planet close by that would be suitable for human life.

Thus the council faces three choices. They can insist that the spaceship be fixed and the colonists from Mars leave and take their chances on finding a suitable planet somewhere close. They can allow the colonists to stay on Nova Terra but insist that they settle on the small island of Parva instead of joining with the settlement on the large continent of Terra Firma. The council must listen to the request of the captain of the spaceship and then discuss the question of what to do with these people. Then they must vote with three of the five agreeing on the same course of action.

The roles to be played are:

Captain. The captain of the spaceship from Mars. He pleads for his people to be allowed full participation in the settlement on Terra Firma. He feels that their chances of finding another planet they could survive on are very small and that there is not enough room on the island of Parva to allow the colonists to live comfortably.

Chaplain. He feels that all of the people must be allowed to stay as part of the settlement on Terra Firma. He thinks all people are part of his responsibility to God.

Successful Farmer. He is opposed to allowing the people to stay at all. He feels that they suffered so much in their first years that others can too. He has several children and wants to leave them a large farm and a bright future. He also thinks that if they allow the Martians to remain the settlement will be overcrowded soon. He does not want his children or grandchildren to have to make the long, dangerous space voyage to find another planet because this one becomes overcrowded. He also does not want to allow them to stay on Parva because he does not think that they will be satisfied there and will try to take over Terra Firma.

Young Farmer. He would like the new colonists to be allowed to stay. He was only a baby when their own ship landed and does not really remember the time of suffering. What he does know is that he is tired of the same small group of people, and he would like to see new people and new things.

Doctor. He would like to forbid the people from staying. He is afraid that they will bring new diseases with them and that the people from his own settlement will get sick because they are not used to the diseases.

Teacher. He would prefer them to stay but keep them on the island of Parva. He thinks that the settlement on Nova Terra needs new ideas since it has been cut off from the rest of the galaxy for so long, but he is afraid that the people from Mars have ways of behaving that would be bad for the people of Nova Terra, so they should be kept to themselves to see what they are like.

3. After the students in each group have discussed the issues and had time to vote, break for a discussion to find out what each group decided. Discuss what people thought they would lose or gain by admitting new people and how the new colonists felt

about the situation. Also, discuss similar situations in American history.

EVALUATION:
Observation of class activities and discussion.

MARGINALITY: MALE AND FEMALE ROLES
(Intragroup Relations)

OBJECTIVES: As a result of this lesson, students should be able to:
1. Relate that the roles of male and female are not the same in all cultures.
2. Conclude that the way men or women behave will be influenced by the time and place in which they live.

METHODS AND MATERIALS:
1. Tell the students that they are to pretend to do some of the things that members of Indian tribes did. The girls are to pretend that they are Indian women and that they are planting gardens or scraping leather. The boys are to pretend that they are getting ready for a ceremonial dance and are painting and decorating themselves.
2. After the activities have gone on for a few minutes, stop the class discussion. Compare the activities of the students with what men and women do today. Discuss who uses makeup today and who does the farming.
3. Tell the students that until recently women were not allowed to vote, and that in fact, in some countries women are still not allowed to vote. Tell them that the class will switch roles with only the girls being allowed to decide things. For the rest of the day every time the class decides something about the class activities or the opinions of the class are requested, allow only the girls to vote or give their opinions.
4. At the end of the day discuss the questions of how it feels to be excluded from decisions simply on the basis of sex and how it feels to exclude others.

EVALUATION:
1. Observe pupil responses during the activities and discussion.
2. Ask the class to write short essays about what they think they would feel like and what they would be interested in doing if they were of the opposite sex.

Index

Aesthetics, 125-127
Affective communication, 7
Affective learning, 87-88
Alienation, 6
Amidon, Edmund, 25, 46
Andersen, Dan, 46
Aschner, Mary Jane, 30
Authority, 146-148

Barnes, Douglas, 56, 61
Bellack, Arno, 14, 15, 19, 20, 22, 35, 42, 46, 61
Bloom, Benjamin, 30, 47, 89
Brogan, D. W., 126, 135
Brubaker, Dale, 86
Bruner, Jerome, 93, 113

Case study strategy, 115-135, 137, 147
   content of, see Case study strategy, topics
   evaluation of, 115
   materials for, 115
   methods of, 115
   objectives for, 115
   purpose of, 115
   summary of, 135
Case study strategy, substantive issues
   example of, 127-130
   transcript and analysis, 130-134
Case study strategy, topics
   aesthetics, 125-127
   classroom life, 116-117
   community life, 120-123
   school life outside of classroom, 116-117
   student health, 123-125
   substantive issues, 127-134
Classroom interaction, see Humanistic instructional behavior, teacher, Humanistic instructional behavior, students, and Humanistic instructional behavior, teacher and students
Clements, H. Millard, 137, 138, 143

Combs, Arthur, 11, 12, 14
Communication, 7, 17-84
Counts, George, 6
Curriculum, definition of, 13

Davis, O. L., 30, 34, 46
Decision-action problems, 138, see also Social action activities
Definitions, types of, 3
Dehumanizing forces, 6
DeVault, M. Vere, 46
Dewey, John, 8
Directions, giving, see Informing behavior, teacher
Dostoevsky, Fyodor, 49, 61

Elzey, Freeman, 40, 42, 46
Environmental pollution, 4, 6, 91, 97-100, 127
Environmental violence, 7
Evaluation, Gestalt games, 110 ff.
Experiential learning, 18

Fielder, William, 143
Flanders, Ned, 25, 46
Freeways, 140-143
Fromm, Erich, 6

Gallagher, James, 30, 34, 46
Gestalt game strategy, 89-113, 137, 140, 146
   adjustment of, 103-110
   definition of, 89
   evaluation of, 110-113
   materials for, 98-103
   methods of, 94-98
   objectives for, 89-94
Gestalt game strategy, lesson plans
   Air Pollution, 162-163
   Authority Representative in Hostile Group, 105
   Back to Nature, 155

City Knowledge, Rural Knowledge, 157-158
Commuter Attitudes, 156
Comparing Cultures, 96-97
Compromise, 3, 174
Compromising, 2, 169-170
Conformity, 175-176
Confrontation with Someone You Dislike, 97-98
Facts and Values, 100-101
Feeling Black, 107
Influencing the Media, 161-162
Information Summarizing, 164-165
Informers in Society, 104-105
Intolerance, 170-174
Landlord-Tenant Confrontation, 95
Loyalty to Community, 157
Marginality: Immigrants, 175
Marginality: Immigrants vs Anglo-Saxon Americans, 106, 176-179
Marginality: Male and Female Roles, 179
Noise Pollution, 165
Overcrowded Territory, 108, 163
Population, 170
Positive Reinforcers: Comments, 168-169
Positive Reinforcers: Smiles and Nods, 166-167
Preferential Treatment, 167-168
Recycling Cans and Paper, 164
Technological Unemployment, 160-161
Trouble in Schools, 158-159
Verbal-Nonverbal Communication, 110-111
Vocations, 108-110
Vocations: Poverty, 159-160
Water Polution, 166

Hamiton, N. K., 10
Hare, R. M., 9
Harmin, Merrill, 47, 61
Harrington, Michael, 7
Huebner, Dwayne, 46
Hughes, Marie, 20, 21, 23, 46, 65, 84
Humanism
  dehumanizing educational practices, 11-12
  humanistic educational practices, 12-13
Humanism, characteristics of, 4-9
  control of destiny, 5
  dignity of man, 4
  emotional and psychological concern, 9
  internationally minded, 8

power-morality issue, 8-9
problem solving, 7-8
qualitative, 9
rational thought, 5
scientific knowledge, 6
social responsibility, 7
Humanism, classical, 5, 7
Humanism, philosophical foundations of, 3-11
Humanistic behavior, meaning of, 14
Humanistic content, see Humanistic subject matter content
Humanistic instructional behavior, students, 49-61, 63-84
  definition of, 49
  qualities of, 49-51
  role reversal, 51
Humanistic instructional behavior, teacher, 17-18, 11-47, 63-84
  criteria for, 17-18
  goals of, 17
Humanistic instructional behavior, teacher and students
  instrument for analysis, 74-75
  relationships between teacher and students, 65-66
  summary of, 63-65
  transcript and analysis of, 66-84
Humanistic qualities, see Human qualities
Humanistic subject matter content, 4, 7-8, 86, 98-100, 115-116 ff, 127, 145
  intergroup relations, 86, 95-98, 99-103, 104-105, 107, 110-111, 127, 166-174
  intragroup relations, 86, 99-100, 106, 127, 174-179
  survival, 86, 99-100, 108-110, 127, 162-166
  technological change, 6, 86, 99-100, 127, 159-162
  urbanization, 6, 7, 86, 99-100, 127, 159-162
Humanistic themes, 89 ff, 155-179
  table of, 99-100
Human qualities, 5, 17, 49-50
Hunter, Elizabeth, 25, 46

Influence, 146-148
Informing behavior, students, 51-55, 63-84
  humanistic criteria of, 52
  humanistic examples of, 52-55
  relating, 54-55

INDEX   183

structuring, 52-54
summary of, 63-64
Informing behavior, teacher, 19-29, 63-84
    concepts for analysis of, 19-21, 25-26
    definition of, 19
    humanistic criteria of, 22-23, 26-28
    humanistic examples of 23-24, 28
    relating, 24-29
    structuring, 19-24
    summary of, 63-64
Inquiry, see Problem solving, Study
Instruction
    definition of, 13
    importance of, 14
    see also Humanistic instructional behavior, teacher
Interaction analysis, see Humanistic instructional behavior, teacher and students
Intergroup relations, 86, 95-98, 99-103, 104-105, 107, 110-111, 127, 166-174
Intragroup relations, 86, 99-100, 106, 127, 174-179

James, William, 10
Johnson, A., 10

Kelley, Earl, 46
Kerner, George, 9
Knowledge problems, 138
Krathwohl, David, 89

Levine, Samuel, 46
Lewis, Wilbert, 25, 46
Liberal arts, 6
Licklider, J. C. R., 113

Macdonald, James, 9-10, 15, 46, 86
Mager, Robert, 90, 113
Masia, Bertram, 89
Materials, Gestalt game strategy of, see Humanistic themes
McLuhan, Marshall, 14, 15
Methods, Gestalt game strategy of, 94-98
Meux, Milton, 25, 31, 34, 46
Moore, G. E., 9

Newall, J. M., 46

Objectives, 90-94, 115
    behavioral, 90-91
    Gestalt games, in, 89-94
    student focus, 93
    subject focus, 92-93
    teacher focus, 91-92
Oliver, Donald, 9, 135

Peirce, Charles, 10
Plato, 7
Pollution, see Environmental pollution
Population, 6, 7, 108, 127
Power, 8-9, 146-148
Praising, see Reacting behavior, teacher
Problem solving, 7, 8, 102
Protagoras, 5

Questioning, see Soliciting behavior, teacher; Soliciting behavior, students

Race relations, 4, 6, 99-102, 104-105, 107, 127-135
Raths, Louis, 42, 47, 50, 61
Reacting behavior, students, 59-61, 63-84
    developing, 60
    humanistic criteria of, 60
    humanistic examples of, 60
    importance of for humanism, 59
    rating, 59-60
    summary of, 65
Reacting behavior, teacher, 39-45, 63-84
    concepts for analysis of, 39-40, 41-42
    definition of, 39
    developing, 40-45
    humanistic criteria of, 43-44
    humanistic examples of, 44-45
    rating, 39-45
    summary of, 65
Responding behavior, students, 57-59, 63-84
    humanistic criteria of, 58
    humanistic examples of, 58
    importance of for humanism, 57-58
    student-student responding, 58-59
    summary of, 64-65
Responding behavior, teacher, 35-38, 63-84
    definition of, 35
    humanistic criteria of, 36-38
    humanistic examples of, 37-38
    summary of, 64-65
    typical responses, 36
Rogers, Carl, 18, 19, 46
Role playing, 147, see also Gestalt game strategy

Sanders, Norris, 30-47
Saylor, J. G., 10
Scheffler, Israel, 3
Schiller, F. C. S., 10
Scientific knowledge, 6
Self-concept, 9
Seligman, E. R. A., 10

Shaftel, Fannie, 94-113
Shaver, James, 9, 135
Simon, Sidney, 47, 61
Smith, B. Othanel, 25, 31, 34, 46
Social action activities, 145-148
  definition of, 145
  examples of, 146-148
  planning of, 148
  rationale for, 145-146
  relationship to information and attitudes, 146-148
Social action activities, types of, 148-151
  bulletin boards, 150
  debates and panel discussions, 149
  door to door interaction, 150
  dramatic presentations, 150
  interviews, 148
  letters, 150
  music compositions, 150
  parent conferences and committees, 150
  photographs, slides, and movies, 149
  poetry, 149
  posters, 149
  public address systems, 149-150
Social responsibility, 7
Sociodrama, see Role playing
Socrates, 9, 50
Soliciting behavior, students, 55-57, 63-84
  humanistic criteria of, 56-57
  humanistic examples of, 57
  importance of for humanism, 55
  increasing students' questions, suggestions for, 56
  summary of, 64
Soliciting behavior, teacher, 29-35, 63-84
  concepts for analysis of, 30-33
  definition of, 29
  humanistic criteria of, 33-34
  humanistic examples of, 34
  summary of, 64
Stevenson, Charles, 9
Strategies, 86
  components of, 86
  definition of, 86
  see also Gestalt game strategy, Case study strategy
  types of, 86
Strategies, humanistic foundations of, 86-88
Study, 137-143
  definition of, 137
  elements of, 137
  examples of, 140-143
  model of, 138-140
  type of problems for, 137-138
Study, model of, 138-140
  acquaintanceship, 138-140
  big question, 138-139, 140
  clarifying and organizing data, 139, 141-142
  data collection, 139, 141-142
  report, 140, 143
  subquestions, 139, 141
Survival, 86, 99-100, 108-110, 127, 162-166

Taba, Hilda, 21, 40, 42, 46
Tabachnick, B. Robert, 143
Teaching, see Instruction
Technological change, 6, 86, 99-100, 127, 159-162
Thomas, R. Murray, 113
Thoreau, Henry, 49, 61
Tinsley, Drew, 30, 34, 46
Toulmin, Stephen, 9

Urbanization, 6, 7, 86, 99-100, 127, 159-162

Value, conflict, 8

War, 127
Whittemore, Richard, 10
Withall, John, 46

Zahorik, John, 39, 41, 42, 47

DISCHARGED
DEC 13 1972
DISCHARGED
DEC 27 1983

DISCHARGED
JUL 14 1973

DISCHARGED
JUL 11 1973
DISCHARGED
MAY 8 1982

DISCHARGED

NOV 28 1988

JUN 27 1974
DISCHARGED
AUG 17 1989

DISCHARGED
MAR 07 1984

DISCHARGED

DISCHARGED
APR 13 1976

DISCHARGED

DISCHARGED
JUN 27 1978

DISCHARGED

DISCHARGED